Among Men

Tobin Siebers **AMONG MEN**

UNIVERSITY OF NEBRASKA PRESS : LINCOLN & LONDON

Copyright © 1998 by the University of Nebraska Press. All rights reserved. Manufactured in the United States of America. A different version of "Knocked Out" appeared in *Michigan Quarterly Review* 36.3 (1997): 457–60.

⊚ The paper in this book meets the minimum requirements of American National Standard for Information Sciences – Permanence of Paper for Printed Library Materials, ANSI Z39.48-1984.

Design: R. Eckersley. Typeset in New Baskerville.

Library of Congress Cataloging in Publication Data
Siebers, Tobin, 1953–
Among men / Tobin Siebers.
p. cm. ISBN 0-8032-4273-5 (cloth : alk. paper)
1. Siebers, Tobin, 1953– . 2. English teachers – United States – Biography. 3. Men – United States – Biography. 4. Men – Psychology. I. Title.
PE64.S44A3 1998 920.71–dc21 98-22577 CIP

Contents

PART 1 MAN KIND AND UNKIND

Catch	3
The Yard	5
Drinking	12
Cicadas	13
Narcolepsy	16
Reading	17
Hardware Men	20
Shaving	24
Heroes	25
The Most Dangerous Creatures	27
The Men of Babel	28
Knocked Out	29

PART 2 FATHER, BROTHER, SON

Dad and the Cops	35
Better Son Than Father	42
Four Men, Four Walls, and a Fire	44
My Mother's Red Shoe	51
Harold Siebers, 1915–1994	52
Packing Up the Tool Box	53
Pictures of My Father	54
The Metaphysics of Lawn Care	56

PART 3 LOVE AND LUST

The Fate of Marriage	59
In Praise of Doris Day	70
Women Are Like the Earth	75
Magic Tricks	76
In the Cave of the Lovers	77
Adam and Eve	78
Lust (Always an Incomplete Story)	79
The Men a Woman Knows	80
In the Metro of the Mind	81

PART 4　　　MAN TO MAN, MOSTLY TO HIMSELF

Teasing 85
Shopping for Time 90
The Mandolins of St. Jean de Luz 92
Anger 98
Grown Men Don't Cry 104
Homunculus 107
Writing Life 111

Part 1: Man Kind and Unkind

Catch

Before my father became too childish to be allowed to travel on planes, trains, or buses by himself, I had my sister pack him off to visit me. I waited for him at the gate. When the plane arrived, I tried to make my way down the ramp to meet him, but the attendants stopped me and made me wait by the door. It was during one of those times when the airline industry was being extra careful about security. My father emerged from the gate alone and in a hurry, with a stewardess trailing him by two minutes.

That afternoon we played catch in the yard. Catch is a simple game that requires more than a usual amount of skill, as anyone who has played catch with a small child knows. But once the skill is there, what pleasure it gives—a pleasure not forgotten when the brain and arm give out. Catch is a conversation without words where repetition and novelty join forces to overpower boredom and fatigue. The repetition gives the game a reassuring certainty. The novelty, which amounts to the small errancy of the ball, is the suspense that keeps the game fresh without jeopardizing its comfort. You know the ball is destined for your hand, and in this knowledge lies the proof that your partner has chosen you above all others. And yet for the ball to reach you requires leaps, stabs, lucky plays. I remember well when I played catch successfully with my son for the first time. It was a small miracle to see him throw the ball into my hands and anticipate the arc of my throw and make his catch.

When evening came, I took my father upstairs for bed. I bathed him in a tub of warm water, toweled his hairy body dry, and helped him into his pajamas. Then I led him into the guest room to tuck him into bed. I pulled the covers up to his chin and leaned over to kiss him good night. Then I said, "Good night, sleep tight, don't let the bedbugs bite." He smiled at me with a wide-eyed grin, suppressing the urge to laugh. His was a deep, childlike contentment similar to what I see on my children's faces at night when they are fully happy and feeling a little impish. But

4   I believe that somewhere beneath several layers of awareness he was laughing at the fact that our roles had become reversed, and he was pleased to be in the care of someone he himself had taught to care.

The Yard

Most American men dislike gardens and really don't know much about them. They are unable to give up the concept of the yard, a vast, policed space where virtue has room to grow in its largest variety and no form of plant life other than grass may intrude. The yard is a velvet carpet rolled out to receive the good life. It stands in readiness to receive romping dogs and children, the idyllic bounce of a baseball, the drop of a noble bat. It is where fathers play catch with children on Saturdays and where mothers steal a few feet of ground along the house to grow geraniums in the summer and tulips in the spring. It is the stage properly set for the arrival of the morning paper, thrown from the careless arm of the paperboy as he speeds by on his bicycle along with the morning sun. It is the domain of the solitary robin, its ear inclined to the earth at day's end, listening for the rumble of worms.

And how convenient is the yard at graduation time! There the proud parents take pictures of the capped and gowned and display the evidence of joy and accomplishment: a cake delicately iced, a shimmering pitcher of pink lemonade, a few gifts well wrapped by the grandparents, a shiny blue convertible parked in the adjacent driveway.

Without the yard these things could not take place. I think most men understand this, and that is why the yard preoccupies them. They have a sacred duty to keep it in a state of readiness, to make it into a proper place where something can grow—not plants or grass but something else: the kind of life Americans still dream about, some in spite of themselves. The yard itself is not the American dream. Nor is it symbolic of this dream. It is the place where the dream can happen. The yard only looks empty. In reality it is a space overflowing with desire. It is maintained in a constant state of readiness to receive the good life, and it provides a standard to measure how deserving a man is of it.

The yard is a place to put things, but if you put something there, the good things in life will have no home when they arrive. The yard is like the extra place and chair set for Elijah at Passover.

6   No one would think of sitting there, and yet true happiness might be achieved if Elijah actually arrived to take his seat. Maybe this explains why men are so concerned with the upkeep of the yard and why most can't abide the thought of turning it over to the women in their life. Men are more at home than women with emptiness. Creatures of desire, they indulge their melancholy by exaggerating the emptiness of their lives, by giving themselves over more and more to what they lack. Only by dwelling on what is missing in one place may they go about trying to fill it up somewhere else, indoors for example. In the yard everything is clear. All is visible. You know what is there and what is not—mostly what is not. On a sunny day, you can see which way the grass grows, and the geometry of the mowing stands out so that the pattern of your life assumes the clarity of a path many times traveled and easily found again.

    I have devoted many hours to the geometry of lawn care. I know the lay of the land in my yard: each slight depression and rise, each old post hole and former bee's nest, each soft spot and stubborn rock. But I have not yet found the best direction to approach them. I continue to experiment with different ways of cutting the grass. Somewhere the perfect pattern exists, and if I can find it, I will be able to set my pace comfortably to the earth where my feet must fall. But there are many obstacles to contend with, even in an empty lot. Mowing works against itself if done badly: the clippings from one cut become an encumbrance to the next. Fences and buildings rise out of the yard and must be cut around, and the edges need to be just right. If you find a pattern, the mowing becomes comfortable, but that doesn't make the pattern right. Clockwise, rectangular cuts are always best for me, but my mower has a side discharge to the right, and so cutting clockwise means that the clippings are sprayed into the path of future cuts. Cutting counterclockwise only works if you start your cut at the center of the lawn, and that makes a man look ridiculous. I have begun to experiment with diagonal cuts, but they really work only if the yard is very geometrical and completely empty, and such is not the case with my yard, with its swing set and irregular checkerboard of grass and concrete patches.

Sometimes in the early evenings, after the heat of the day has died down, I join the army of men who march into the yard and fill the air with the sounds of mowing. The roar of power mowers blends together without dissonance, so that the work of my neighbor becomes indistinguishable from my own. I concentrate on the stretch of ground before me, trying to fathom it: to grasp the direction of the grasses, to measure the minute elevation of climb or descent, to bring all of my observations together into the perfect survey of my property so that I might put this knowledge to good use and understand once and for all in what direction, in what pattern, I might approach my mowing. As I drive the mower forward, making sharp turns and backing over errors in judgment, I think of the virtues of pure geometry, composing curvilinears in my head, plotting triangulations, and divining the hypotenuse.

I am distrustful of men who turn their yard work over to their wives or children. They are either lazy or weak or both. "Man of the house" is a misnomer because the man of the house should be in charge only of the yard. He may turn some of the work over to his sons or daughters to help build their character or bank account, but no one else, especially not his wife, has any business cutting his lawn, except in case of emergency. It doesn't matter if she likes to mow and he doesn't. Mowing is not something you do because you like it; its pleasures lie elsewhere, in the contemplation of an open space well framed or in the thought of having done what was right to do.

I know these opinions are out of date and unpopular. They don't fit with my other opinions, and I have no idea where I got them. Nor do I know for fact whether they are widely shared by other men, but I suspect they are, because I don't know a self-respecting man who behaves otherwise.

I am a modern man and I tolerate a certain level of technology. I would not think of using a push mower, for example, even though power mowers are even more ecologically unsound than refrigerators. Labor-saving devices such as handheld leafblowers and edgers are too fussy for me, and they lack the simple dignity of rakes, shovels, and hoes. What does it mean to save yourself from labor anyway? What do you do after you have been saved? Probably play golf—a game whose entire purpose is to reach a small patch of grass so perfectly manicured that a little dimpled ball can roll upon it unobstructed. Golf is not a game for golfers at all. Golfers are only lawn ornaments that exist solely for the enjoyment of greenskeepers. The greenskeepers already possess in minute detail the knowledge of geometry and ground, of incline and curve, of height and distance that defines the game of golf. I imagine them sitting on a shady hill after a day's work in the meadows, smiling at the ornamental flags and markers, the flight of the ball and its graceful bounce, the colorful jerseys of the golfers who meander in their foursomes from green to green as if performing for the pleasure of kings.

The most important thing for a man is to pick something hard to do and then find the best way to do it—not the easiest way, not the shortest way. The best way. Only then is he assured of having some time on his hands.

All children in middle America, at least those of my time, remember the yard where they first grew up. My first yard was on a street called Eden. The yard on Eden Avenue was overrun with clover, and I seem to remember at least a dandelion or two, if they are ever so solitary. My father once went so far as to change the entire landscape of the yard by bringing in three truckloads of dirt and flattening it out with a large metal barrel filled with water. The children had the privilege of riding on it to increase the weight. My father's efforts changed the lay of the land but not what grew on it, and I think he learned his lesson. Afterward, his only comment on the yard, aside from indulging his fireman's complex in the evenings, was to threaten to pave it over and paint it green. I summon these memories whenever my preoccupation with the yard threatens to turn into an obsession.

Over the years I have engaged in a gentle competition with my neighbors over our lawns. I have never been close to winning, but neither have I ever finished in last place. I am happy in moderation. The first prize always goes to the retired furnaceman on the corner, whose eye is so clear that he can detect the intention of crabgrass to take up residence. He crawls on hands and knees over the surface of his yard with garden tools on the hip. He is a geometer of fine sensibilities.

A few years ago another neighbor decided to up the ante. He hired a lawn company to tear out his entire lawn and replant it from scratch. He didn't like the idea of using chemicals and didn't have the stamina to weed. I had always liked his lawn because it had a gentle growth of wildflowers in the spring, and the grass was fine and didn't grow too fast. The lawn company men arrived with their tractor and tools and rolled the lawn up like a carpet. After much raking and commotion, they brought in a tanker and sprayed the lot with a slurry of seed, fertilizer, and green papier-mâché. The paper acts like straw and stores moisture for the seedlings. They say you can grow a lawn with it even in the hottest days of July and August. Sure enough, real grass soon came in, and my neighbor began to take up a defensive posture, roping off the yard and hanging do-not-tread signs about. Up to that point, I had really taken the whole thing very well. In fact, I found it amusing. But the hint of his success brought out the criminal in me. I imagined an act of vandalism: I would harvest the dandelions from my own yard and under cover of darkness, after performing a ritual dance to the god Weed, I would scatter them over his front yard. Then I would lie back in wait for the poison to spread, and on some future Saturday afternoon as he stood despondent over his lawn, I would cross the street to commiserate with him about the vanity of trying to defeat Mother Nature.

My fantasies remained only fantasies, as did his. The next spring, wildflowers sprouted as usual. At first I thought he had replanted them, but I later discovered they were the reason for his original travail. I am happy to report that the lawn company chose the variety of grass best suited to his shady lot, which is to say, the variety that was already growing there. His yard today looks much as it always did: a loose and fine growth of grass capped in the spring by the purple foam of wildflowers.

It is difficult to romanticize lawn care. The yard is most often a subject of parody or satire: the pink flamingo lawn ornament is a universal symbol of the bad taste and kitschy desire of people who cultivate their lawns. I have never understood, however, how one can be so unromantic about yards and so thoroughly romantic about gardens. It is true that flowers have a certain appeal to the heart. One would expect, however, that some seven hundred years of doting on roses and their relation to love would impair the symbolism, and people would grow sick of sweeping up dead petals. With the decline of flower power, the lawn should be a welcome innovation in the language of love. It is a neater symbol of desire, possessing all the old properties of love's decline but in subtler degree: the grass grows dull and withdrawn if not properly cared for, instead of falling dramatically to pieces. It is as multifaceted and as myriad as the moments that make up a romance, and yet it is a single entity. It is fragile, being subject to conquest by riffraff and adulterous strangers, and its verdure exudes freshness and sexual vigor. Grass is certainly more hospitable to romance than the rose. Try reclining with your beloved in a rose garden and then compare it to making love on the lawn, and you will discover to your relief that the grass is no bed of roses.

Our finest poet of the yard is John Cheever, whose stories find their proper setting and true romance on the boxy, spacious lawns of modern suburbia. In "The Swimmer," the yards of the neighborhood are joined by a circuit of swimming pools, and the hero has the idea of swimming across the county to his home. When he finally arrives, his house is empty of family and furniture. In the film version, Burt Lancaster refuses to enter the front door and crouches half-naked and shivering next to his porch under the eaves. "The Chimera" tells of a henpecked husband banished by his homicidal wife to the yard, the bathroom, and the corners of rooms. He imagines in his desperation a woman so ardently unreal that he stands in the rain for an hour talking to her before returning wet to the skin to the kitchen. When the mermaid leaves him to return home, he realizes that her parting only means that she has made room for someone else and he may now people his imagination with other beauties: melancholy brunettes, lonely housewives, sloe-eyed dancers. But the story is not really about the kinds of women imagined by the hero; it is about all the empty places in his life that need to be filled, and among these, the yard is the most vivid and vacant. I love John Cheever's stories and I am grateful for them. And yet his vision is somehow too disheartening, perhaps too much the reflection of his own private despair, without enough solitude for my taste. I prefer my yard to remain empty of everything but my desire to have it filled. In my yard, I meet no mermaid out of her element who wanders across my lawn from the pages of a romance, her perfect hair and body interfering with the real harmony of my creation. No. I dream of no such fleshy embodiments of the good life. I stand, a lonely sentinel at the center of the geometrical pattern cut by the tracks of my power mower, my spatula ready in salute before my Weber grill, polished to an ecstatic ebony, as the smoke of cooking meat rises in perfect vertical ascent toward the ceiling of the property, where it breaks off at a right angle to join the smoke trails of every other guardian of the neighborhood, each stream of exhaust migrating in a vast field of parallel lines toward the final destination.

Drinking

Men sometimes fill up their emptiness with drink. Bottles and bottles of beer, sometimes barrels of it, glasses of whisky and wine, gin, and vodka are poured methodically into the emptiness. The arm becomes a machine to serve the throat. The throat is not dry or thirsty. The drinking satisfies the craving of the arm to fill the throat. Thirst choked becomes desire quenched.

Once after a long night at a bar, during which I had felt at any number of times that I was too tired to go on, my drinking partner and I suddenly found our second wind and bought a six-pack of beer at last call. We carried it away from the bar and down the hill to the river, where we laid ourselves out on the riverbank and continued to talk and drink, not wanting to see the night end, finding in its vast emptiness enough peace of mind to keep us there beside the water.

Cicadas

Gloudeman's Pond lay two miles and three trestles down the railroad tracks from our neighborhood. You can't fall through the railroad ties on a trestle, but it always feels like you might, so I was nervous whenever the neighborhood boys went on an expedition to the pond. We went often because it offered irresistible attractions: frogs and crayfish in dizzying numbers, and every once in a while a big sand turtle sunning itself on a black floating log. The other boys said there were snappers there, too. The only thing about Gloudeman's Pond was that you had to watch your step. Even though I never saw a single cow there, the pasture was covered with cow pies.

One day five of us made the trip down the rails to the pond. We hadn't brought fishing gear. We didn't have string and liver, so we couldn't catch crayfish. We always got the liver from the butcher shop at the Red Owl. The butcher let us have all we wanted without asking one red cent for it. We'd tie a chunk of liver to some string and drop it into the pond. The crayfish attacked the bait and gripped it with their claws so stubbornly that you could just haul them in and drop them into a milk carton. But we didn't have any liver that day. We were just hanging around, chasing each other through the pasture. It was a very hot day, and we were working up a sweat. Suddenly a tremendous screeching came at us from a big maple tree. Everyone stopped and listened. Then Dave and George scooped up some gravel from the tracks and threw it in handfuls at the maple. Soon Denny and Paul started to throw stones, too. Finally, I joined in, and the five of us pelted the maple something fierce. The stones flew into its branches, shredding the leaves and ricocheting off the limbs. Stones and leaves rained down from the tree to the ground. "It's a good thing," I kept thinking, "that this tree doesn't belong to anyone. It's a good thing this isn't somebody's lawn. It's a good thing nobody's here." But I threw the gravel anyway.

Then something flew down from the tree. It looked like a maple seedling or a dragonfly zigzagging to the ground. We stopped throwing rocks and ran over to it. It was a cicada—green and shiny, almost transparent, with luminous wings that looked wet in the sunlight. Its head was enormous. It had a small stout body. And its eyes were closed tightly. It reminded me of the skull and crossbones on the iodine bottle in our medicine cabinet at home, and I was afraid it would fly up at me. But it just sat there, its eyes closed tightly and its wings twitching in the sun. We circled around it, bent over it peering down, and then suddenly it hopped. We all jumped back except Dave, our leader. In a flash he was on it, stamping it into the ground. The cicada was dead, the broad head smashed, the wings twisted and bent. Dave poked at it with a stick and turned it over. I thought it would have a thousand legs but it didn't. Then he skewered it with the stick and picked it up. He dangled it around on the end of the stick and jabbed it at George. George jerked his head back and his eyeglasses flipped off, but he held his ground. Then Dave poked it at me. I jumped back, and he began to chase me with it. "I'm going to drop it down your shirt," he shouted. I ran away and the other boys ran after me. George and Denny were yelling, "Drop it down his shirt!" "Drop it down his shirt!" So Dave kept screaming, "I'm going to drop it down your shirt." I raced across the pasture with the four of them swarming behind me, but I couldn't get away. They had me. I swerved to the side and slipped right into a juicy cow platter. I slid to the ground and fell on the seat of my pants right in the wet shit. My trouser leg worked like a scoop, and the green shit was packed up my pant leg from ankle to knee.

The boys all laughed. They heckled me and danced around the other cow pies, pretending to step in one and then jumping away. Dave said, "God, he stinks! Let's get out of here!" George said it, too, "Yeah, he stinks!" Then they took off in a pack, running as fast as they could.

I got up and chased after them. But I was covered with cow shit and I couldn't catch up. I tried to shake it off as I ran. "Wait up! Wait up!" I yelled. But if they heard me, they weren't listening. I ran after them for a long time. I knew they were heading for Dave's house. They kept running down the tracks, and every once in a while they would look back and then run away faster. I had to cross the three trestles by myself. I could see the water through the tracks. I thought I would fall between the greasy black timbers or get an ankle stuck and break it, but I made it by jumping from tie to tie.

When I got to Dave's house, the yard was empty. There was no grass growing in the yard on the side of his house because the maple trees were too dense. It was like a huge cave or tunnel, with the house on one side and a line of trees on the other. I ran around the house a few times looking for my friends. I called at the door. I jumped up and down, trying to look into the windows to see if anyone was inside the house. I went into the garage to see if Dave and the guys were hiding there. But I couldn't find anyone.

Everything was quiet. I stood on the damp mud in the shelter of the maples next to the house. It was as if I were all alone in the clearing of an immense forest. It was warm and humid, the leaves above were scratching at each other, and the sunlight filtered through the dark green canopy of the branches, casting strange yellow-blue lines across the clearing. I thought about the other boys. I could sense their breathing. I could feel them laughing at me. I knew they were there somewhere. I dropped my chin down to my chest and let my arms fall limply to my sides. I squeezed my eyes shut and strained to hear them.

At first I couldn't hear a thing. Then I heard my blood moving in my ears. I thought about the cicada lying on the ground with its eyes closed tightly and its wings twitching at its sides. I thought about all the other cicadas in the world.

Narcolepsy

I learned to speak French in southern France in Avignon, where I lived for a summer with Monsieur and Madame Deshors and their twenty-year-old daughter. Monsieur Deshors was a narcoleptic. Almost every night after eating, we would all sit down to play cards at the dining-room table. We would play for an hour or two, until Monsieur Deshors's eyes abruptly fell shut and he passed out. Then Madame Deshors would announce the end of the game, rouse her husband, and lead him off to bed. One night Madame Deshors and her daughter decided they were going to go to the movies. They wanted to see Paul Mazursky's *An Unmarried Woman*. We ate dinner, and then the ladies did the dishes, put on their twin red coats, and left the apartment. As soon as they were out the door, Monsieur Deshors asked me if I was hungry, even though we had just finished a big meal. We went into the kitchen, where he made two enormous roast beef sandwiches and drew two cold beers out of the refrigerator. We carried the beer and sandwiches out to the balcony, which overlooked the back of the building, the rear alley, and many, many red tile roofs. We stood on the balcony eating the sandwiches and drinking the beers for a long time. It was as if we were eating and drinking in slow motion, as if the sandwiches were as big as pillows and the beers, bottomless. He told me about his life, about how his business had come to an end and he had taken another job. He told me about his son's life and the lives of his son's friends, about his daughter at home and his daughter away from home, about his marriage, about the furniture in the house, about cars he had owned and the cars he wanted to own. When Madame Deshors and her daughter returned near midnight, we were still standing on the balcony, looking out over the red tile roofs of the city. Monsieur Deshors had not fallen asleep. Now when I think back on that night, it seems like I was the one who fell asleep, and maybe I was dreaming.

Reading

To read, you have to have already begun to have read. I know this is not a very readable sentence. But don't abandon me yet. Scale back your expectations and remember what it was like to learn to read. Remember your first-grade reader? Dick and Jane and Spot and all the running about? Remember what it was like to pick up a third-grade reader by accident? Or to come upon a piece of print, lying on the living-room floor or blowing along the pavement? It was like coming upon the Rosetta stone or being hit by a moon rock, fallen to planet earth. It was an experience of panic and wonderment and dizziness: an ear-ringer, a head-cracker, a brain-bewilderer. So to read, you have to have already begun to have read. It is a gradual process, one of accumulation, of joining letter to letter, syl•lab•i•cal•ly, to make a word, a sentence, a paragraph, and then a meaning.

When I was in the sixth grade, my sister, who was then in college and possessed an arch sense of humor, gave me a copy of Djuna Barnes's *Nightwood* to read. I knew most of the words and I read it, but I didn't understand it. When on the last page Robin got down on all fours next to her canine friend and whimpered like a dog, it gave me a headache. But, then, I had the same experience when I first read *Mad* magazine in the fourth grade. At that time, I was reading mostly *Superman* comic books, and picking up *Mad* was like stumbling upon a piece of kryptonite. I was just not prepared for it.

I have read all the novels of Dostoyevsky. He is a talented "writer," or perhaps "talker" is the better description for him. Dostoyevsky is one of the great writers who didn't always write. He dictated a few of his novels, and someone else, his wife or someone who was about to become his wife, wrote down the words. When you read *Crime and Punishment* and realize that parts of it are a bundle of inspired talk, it stirs the greatest admiration and awe. That is, until you read Tolstoy, who didn't dictate his novels but wrote them. Tolstoy's sentences are crafted in the mind's eye with a regard worthy of the world and its timeless measure, while Dostoyevksy's sentences, even the written ones, obey the wild cadences of a voice fearful of the future and wretched over the past. Now, as I said, I have read all the novels of Dostoyevsky. But I can't make the same claim about Tolstoy. Dostoyevsky is the first-grade reader that prepares you for the third-grade reader, and for my money, Tolstoy is the third-grade reader. It is not unusual in the cast of characters of a novel by Tolstoy to come upon someone who resembles Dostoyevsky, but Dostoyevsky was not up to the task of creating a character as original as Tolstoy. That is the real difference between them.

I've read *Anna Karenina* many times, and whenever I go on a long trip or spend a year abroad, I take the novel with me so I can read it again. I also take *War and Peace* with me, but I have never been able to read it. I have started it on a number of occasions, but I have never gotten far enough into it to be able to pretend I have read it, even under pressure, when my self-respect is on the line. I have a feeling for the atmosphere of the novel, but my familiarity is like that given by standing in the antechamber of a great cathedral: I peer into its depths, glimpse the merging of sunlight and shadows, but I am not allowed to enter. I can only conclude that I have not yet read enough to be worthy of it.

My current project is to read everything I can lay my hands on so I will be able to muster the strength to read *War and Peace*. Jane Austen—a walk in the park. The complete works of the Marquis de Sade—child's play. The *Standard Edition* of Freud— no sweat. Hegel's *Phenomenology of Spirit*—nothing to it. I think, "Now I'm in shape. I'm ready for some heavy lifting." But Tolstoy is too heavy.

For a while, when I was younger, I thought Dostoyevsky was superior to Tolstoy. I read *Brothers Karamazov* and thought about joining the priesthood. When I told my girlfriend about it, she took it personally and wouldn't speak to me for a week. Fortunately, the afterglow of the novel lasted only a few days, and I was spared the monastic life. Then I read *Resurrection*, Tolstoy's novel about prison life. Tolstoy never spent a day in jail. Dostoyevsky served hard time in the Tsar's prison fortress. But Tolstoy's descriptions of the prison world are superior to Dostoyevsky's. They are more vivid, more real, and more true, and Tolstoy only wrote the novel to make some quick cash for friends (who didn't even have the good sense to accept it). Over the years people have talked combustibly to me about their love for Dostoyevsky. Great Books courses often climax with him; he turns up frequently on book lists used in university curriculums. College courses never seem to include Tolstoy, not even one of the short works. Students usually think that he is an old fogy, passé, a strange relic—like a saint's elbow—incomprehensible to our world.

Now when young men or women tell me they like Dostoyevsky but can't read Tolstoy, I tell them to keep reading Dostoyevsky until they have had enough practice to read Tolstoy.

War and Peace stares at me from my bookshelf. There is a wooden shelf, which holds my most precious books, suspended over the radiator next to my desk. The carpenter who made it—obviously a man of limited talents—didn't build the shelf flush to the wall, so a large gap opens between the edge of the shelf and the wall of the building. Of all my books, only *War and Peace* is broad enough to straddle the abyss between the bookshelf and the outside world. It holds that honored position—a solid object, impenetrable to the eye of this reader, awaiting a stronger vision. Perhaps that carpenter was a craftsman after all—and a reader of Tolstoy. He knew no bookshelf could hold him, so he designed a way to suspend him in midair.

Hardware Men

Mike is my hardware man. He works in a full-service hardware on the beltline near my house. It is the most unlikely place for a good hardware—or so I imagine—since I envision the good hardware store as existing only at the center of town. I stumbled into the place one day on a hunch. After driving by many times, I happened to notice that the parking lot was crowded with pickups and professional panel trucks—a very good sign for a hardware store. So I ventured in, and what to my wondering eyes should appear but five guys in plaid shirts and penny nails in the rear. Everything was for sale by item and weight, and everything was there.

A few weeks later I returned with a problem in hand. I was changing a washer in a faucet on my kitchen sink. The bibb screw that holds the washer in place had broken off, and there wasn't enough of it exposed to catch my pliers. I took the whole works in, wrapped in a rag in my pocket, and began to scout the store for the top dog. He was standing in the corner telling a customer how to install a $4.79 single-pole rotary dimmer switch. The guy was taking notes on a scrap of paper. I lined up behind him, and when my turn came I pulled the faucet stem out of my pocket and showed it to the man whom the other guys sometimes called "Mikey" but whom I have always called "Mike." He took one look at it and waved me into the back room. He put the stem in the vise, drilled out the old bibb screw, and retapped the hole. This took fifteen minutes. Then he led me over to the wall and showed me where he kept the brass machine screws. He fished the right size out of the bin with thumb and middle finger, tapped it into the hole, and gave it a twist to set it. "Voilà," he said, like no Frenchman ever had. All I could do was nod my head in agreement.

The screw cost 6 cents. The labor was free, of course, because I was in a hardware store. When I didn't have the penny, he rang up the sale for a nickel. At that moment I became a customer for life. I buy everything I need there and many things I don't need.

If Mike says something is good to have around, I buy it, because a man can never have too many good things around the house.

Where lesser men have failed, Mike has come through for me. I had a plumber in one day to unplug the drain in the laundry room tub. The fit was too tight to get my plunger over the drain. I couldn't use my snake because the nut on the sink trap was frozen. I had to resort to chemicals, and they didn't work. The plumber was a massive man who could barely sidle down the stairs into my basement. He looked over the job, climbed back up to his truck, and reappeared with a miniature toilet plunger that looked like a toy. With pinkie finger daintily extended, he set the plunger over the drain and gave it a little push. Whoosh! Down the drain went the standing water. Price tag: 53 bucks!

Of course, while he was there, I directed him to all the problems I had been saving up. One was my upstairs toilet. It is a unique design, so unique that no replacement parts are available. The threads had worn off the lift wire connected to the tank ball. I had jerry-rigged another lift wire, but the assembly was wrong and the ball fell erratically. The plumber took one look and told me I would have to replace the entire toilet if I wanted something that flushed.

The next Saturday I pulled the beast apart, put its insides into a pan, and went to see Mike. We took a turn down the plumbing aisle to confirm what he already knew—there were no replacement parts to match what I needed. There in the aisle, incidentally, was that little toy plunger for $1.09. The store catalog showed nothing was available in parts' heaven, so I was on my own in the netherworld of home repair. But a worthy guide was leading me. We laid out on the counter all the ballcocks and flush valves he had and managed to patch together several systems, which given a lot of imagination and the proper adjustment might fit together and might even work. I struggled at home for the rest of the afternoon with the jigsaw puzzle. Then I turned on the water, filled the tank, and gave it a flush. "Voilà," as Mike would say. Total cost: $12.48 including tax.

The hardware man is an endangered species because his natural habitat is being destroyed. Something greater in magnitude but not greater in virtue is replacing the hardware store: the modern hardware warehouse. As I roam through these new hardware citadels, I am amazed by the sheer size of the space and the quantity of the goods. The buildings are a full three stories high, not less than 100,000 square feet, and stacked to the roof and walls with products. But more amazing than their size is the absence of people who see your problem as their problem. I go on safari to find a hardware man, combing the aisles for a colorful uniform. I know better than to look for the trademark plaid shirt worn by the hardware man of yesteryear. The new breed of hardware man is a specialist, and he needs a special outfit. When I pin one down, I discover he is one of many assistant managers. He has to read the labels on the shelves to see what an item is. He has no idea what it does or what it can be made to do by a skillful hand.

In the surrounding aisles hang packages and packages of parts—"assortments" they call them. Assortments force you to buy in quantity and in kinds you will never need. For every two ¼ rubber beveled faucet washers, the package also includes two 00, 0, ¼L, and ⅜ washers. The ten washers and three different bibb screws cost $1.97. In other words, to replace the washers in three sets of faucets, you will need to buy three packages of assortments for a grand total of $5.91 plus tax. The extra twenty-four washers lie on your workbench, doomed to depressive uselessness, because it is rare in a well-built house to find faucets that require more than one or two sizes of washer.

Another innovation concocted by the hardware warehouse is the repair kit. Repair kits play the same trick on you as assortments. They always include everything you would need if you had to repair everything that could possibly go wrong. But since everything rarely goes wrong, you end up buying a lot of spare parts you will never use.

A good hardware store can have nothing to do with assortments or repair kits. They are the enemies of precision, ingenuity, and thrift, which are the virtues of the good craftsman. But being good is becoming exceedingly expensive these days, and people can no longer afford it. Or, perhaps, there isn't enough goodness left in the world to sustain places like hardware stores. It doesn't take a mathematical genius or a hardware man to figure out that you can't pay a man enough money to support his family if he is going to take half an hour to sell a 6-cent bibb screw for a nickel. So even though that one little screw is all you need, you are going to have to buy an assortment of screws for 78 cents to get it. That is the wave of the future in the hardware business and everywhere else.

    I will miss the hardware store when it is gone. The hardware man is man at his finest. All that matters to him is that you're trying to fix something. That is enough to make you a member of his club. He will help you even though he doesn't know you. He will teach you even though you're unteachable. He will do it all for practically nothing because he believes things need to be done. You have come into his store because you share his creed. Otherwise, you wouldn't be there asking dumb questions.

Shaving

One day, after I had enough of a beard to make shaving every day a routine and had done it enough to have developed some theories about how to do it, my father happened into the bathroom and saw me putting my theories into practice. Even though it was not his face, he showed me how to do it the right way: soak my face with hot water for a long time, at least as long as it would take me to shave, gather up hot lather from a bar of soap and rub it into my face, rinse off the soap and lather up a second time before taking the blade to my face. He taught me I should cut upwards on my left side and downwards on my right side and with the grain on my lower neck.

He knew my face pretty well. It was the face of his first-born son, and he had been staring into it since my birth, when pushing whiskers was years away. He had gazed into that face and imagined the growth of a future beard, first a fuzzy blond, then a curly dark brown with flicks of red, later turning to a straight wiry gray. The face lost its flatness as the flesh seeped out from under it, leaving the skin hanging loosely over the jawbone—a jawbone he knew well because he had run a piece of sharp steel over one like it every day of his life.

I have followed my father's advice about shaving all these years as if I invented it myself. It has come in handy when I want to feel clean.

Heroes

The most cowardly man owns tales handmade for the life of a hero, tales where he has tried to save a life, where a gun has come out of a drawer, where he has seen a knife flash within an inch of his life. These tales may be real or imagined, but they are necessary to his self-conception. For it is hard to think of yourself as a man without possessing at least some measure of heroism.

My first and, I hope, last knife fight happened in the late seventies in a bar in Wisconsin. To get things straight, he had the knife. I didn't. I didn't pick it up when I had the chance. A short but tough-looking man was playing a bowling game near the bar with some regulars. I was sitting behind them at the bar in a corner with a friend. Something happened at the game, and the short guy pulled a six-inch hunting knife from his belt holster and began to menace the other two men. He was fairly tipsy, however, and at one point when he was gesturing with the knife it flew out of his hand and slid past me on the floor into the corner. He turned to run for it, and although I had the distance in my favor, I didn't go for the knife when I jumped off my stool but tried to block his way to it instead. It occurred to me too late that I should have gone for the knife and tossed it over the bar. He knocked me to one side, picked up the knife, and turned on me. "Do you want a taste of this?" he asked. I raised my hands to wave him off, and he pushed past me and went to his place at the bar. The next night I read in the police and fire beat that a man fitting his description had stabbed someone two hours later.

What is it about men that makes them think they have to do battle, that they have to save the world? You can read accounts daily of men who throw themselves in harm's way simply because they can't help themselves. There can be no other explanation. And for every man who does the deed, there are probably twenty who imagine themselves doing it.

Perhaps a man doesn't have to be a hero, although it might

be necessary for him to imagine himself as one from time to time if he is ever to be happy. I do know a man needs to be somebody, and often this means feeling he has done something good when no one else would.

The Most Dangerous Creatures

Men play at everything when they are among men. They play at everything until they get serious, and then nothing can get them to be playful again but the passage of time. Then they reveal themselves for what they are. Men are the most dangerous creatures on the face of the earth. Their minds are factories for killing. Walter Mitty dreamed about massacring Tyrannosaurus rex by the thousands. The murderous T-Rex never had such thoughts. Most living things exist in fear of men, and those that don't will soon be wiped out. Then the only man-eaters left on earth will be men.

When I was a young man, I lived in Baltimore for a few years. I was applying for my first passport and had to go downtown to have the photographs taken. I dressed up in my very best clothes, took the bus downtown to the harbor area, found the photographer's place, and he took some pictures. He told me to come back for them in thirty minutes. I walked to a nearby park and sat down on a bench to wait. After a few minutes, another man sat down on the bench. He was big and poor. I took him for a man living on the streets. He asked me what it was like to work for the government. I told him I was a student. He asked me whether I had any money. I told him I didn't. He asked me, "What if I have a knife in my coat? What if I take it out and cut you?" I said to him, "Then I will bleed." He looked at me for a while without taking his eyes off me. Then he stood up and left me sitting by myself on the bench.

The Men of Babel

There is something missing from the story of the Tower of Babel. It is the fact that men find pleasure in ruin. The men of Babel decided to raise a tower to rival the might of God. The tower was a staircase to the heavens made to allow the men to knock uninvited at the gates of paradise, to throw open God's door, to run riot in his house. God grew angry at their insolence and cursed them with many tongues so they could not work together. The din of their mangled talk rose up to heaven and pleased God. Below, the men of Babel worked to complete the tower but to no avail. As they piled stone upon stone and despaired at their ineptitude, the tower became more and more unsteady and began to fold in the wind. The men fell back in fear and awe as they watched it crash to the ground. Then, unexpectedly, like mischievous little boys playing with building blocks, they began to exchange smiles and chortle, cavorting among the fallen stones and rolling on the ground. They laughed their heads off at the chaos and sought out each stone that remained atop another stone and knocked it down into the dust. God heard the howls of laughter and looked down in horror at the men of Babel. And so God was defeated after all, because he brought ruin upon the men of Babel but could take no pleasure in it.

Knocked Out

For several years, before I reached my early teens, I had a crew cut, like all the other boys in the neighborhood. The fifties were still in the air, although it was already the sixties, and boys wore white T-shirts and crew cuts. But almost overnight, in the space of one short summer, I had to grow my hair out because my skull got as scarred as the mangy hide of an old dog. The scars on my head have been hidden now for many years, but I still remember where they are and where they came from, because a blow to the head is not something you forget—even if it makes you forget yourself for a while.

Over my right ear on the cusp of my skull I was poked one morning with a long iron bar. The boy down the block was the grandson of a mason, like me, and we were playing next to his grandfather's truck. The truck held a snarl of nubbly iron bars, some straight as sticks, others crossed like pretzels. The men threw them down before pouring cement to reinforce the concrete and to make the roads last a long time. Bill climbed into the back of the old black pickup truck. I started to climb up, too. Bill said it was his grandfather's truck and I couldn't come up. When I didn't listen, he tried to get my attention by picking up one of the straight iron bars. Then he reinforced his point by poking me in the head with it. The old eight ball spun on my shoulders and I went down into a dark pocket full of stars. I remember getting up. By that time, Bill was in the next yard, looking on with a little dread and more curiosity, his arms crossed over his chest. I decided to go home. My mother came to the door when I knocked, probably thinking I was a door-to-door salesman, and then her face fell at the sight of me standing there, a hole in my head, my ear full of gravel and blood, the right sleeve of my white T-shirt soaked red at the shoulder. I think I finally came to when I saw her see me.

A few weeks later Bill gave me some smoked fish to taste for the first time. Then he hit me on top of the head with the safe end of a claw hammer. You can't really see the top of your own head, even in a mirror, so I had to imagine the hammer mark stamped on my skull—I saw it as a cross between a whale's blowhole and the half moon made in a pine board when the hammer misses the nail. Another time, we were arguing near his mother's flower bed next to the house when I turned to walk away. He hit me with a red clay brick, this time from behind. The blow drove my forehead into the side of their imitation sandstone house—double whammy. Tiny leaves, smaller than an infant's hand, fell from the trees in front of me and floated past the shining windows of the neighborhood houses. I woke up face down in a pile of crushed hollyhocks, my least favorite flower to this day.

Time flies when you're unconscious, but unconsciousness does have its season. I remember devoting a lot of attention to it at a certain age, and every other boy I knew felt the same way. It was part of playing army or cowboys and Indians. It seemed like something a man needed to know how to do, as if the thickness of his skull was one proof of manhood, as if a man needed to be knocked out to prove he could get back up and fight again. My brother and I were always pretending to take blunt instruments to one another's head: the handle of a toy revolver or a rifle butt, a skillful right cross followed by the joyful cry, "You're knocked out!" When the James Bond fad arose, karate chops to the back of the neck became a favorite method for dispatching an enemy. There was always a special glee in playing Superman because no matter how hard the blow, he couldn't be knocked out, though we did contrive situations where Clark Kent had to feign unconsciousness.

The movies and television we watched pictured hero after hero who could take a blow to the head and shake it off with a snarl. Each one had his particular technique for dealing with the knockout. When John Wayne was hit, his habitual swagger turned a lazy waltz step while he held the back of his neck and gave his head a defiant toss or two. Humphrey Bogart always had a cigarette as soon as he came to. The fire in his nostrils worked like smelling salts. Duke and Bogie were hard to knock out, usually requiring an extra kick in the head once they were down, and they woke up quickly and with all their instincts alive and ready for action. Of course, the bums and bad guys always went down with a daisy punch; their lights were out before they hit the ground, and they never got up again.

All knockouts, imagined or real, fascinated us. We followed boxing and studied its techniques. We knew we were destined to enter a world where men played rough with each other and where you had to be able to take terrible blows. The image of an enraged and jubilant Cassius Clay standing over the paralyzed body of Sonny Liston transfixed us. The men in the neighborhood couldn't stop talking about it either. The invisible punch, they called it. Moments into the first round, Liston's head butted up against an invisible anvil and he toppled to the canvas, knocked cold but still twitching from the punch.

Every day we waited with eagerness for the violence of the male world to reach out for us. Our small town was full of veterans who hobbled around telling stories about the Battle of the Bulge. We saw our fathers get teeth knocked out at work or lose fingers and hands and feet to the grinding machinery of the mill.

And so we practiced being knocked out whenever we had the chance. When Bill wasn't knocking me out with one of his grandfather's tools, I was knocking myself out. It was also the summer of the intentional knockout. The boys in the neighborhood had perfected a method: you hyperventilated and then on "Go!" sucked in your breath while another boy lifted you in a bear hug off the ground. The surrounding gang would count to ten while you held your breath, but you usually passed out before the ten count, and if you didn't, you surely did on the next try. Sometimes the boys with watches timed how long you were out. Then we had competitions to stay under the longest. Once when I woke up nobody was there. Everybody was hiding in the bushes.

As turn followed upon turn, we grew giddier and our antics with the unconscious boy got increasingly daring and dangerous. You'd wake up in embarrassing positions. Dog shit mustaches were much in vogue. They'd deposit you on a porch, ring the doorbell, and run away. Then it happened. The amateur undertaker squad was moving Bobby Ringo to some ideally prankish location when we accidentally dropped him on the asphalt. I was watching, not carrying, and I saw the boys flip him over for a better grip and then lose the handle. I yelled "Watch out!" but it was too late. Bobby's brain smacked the asphalt hard. A goose egg appeared on his forehead immediately, and he didn't come to for a long time. We got his mother. The doctor was called. He had a concussion and didn't come out to play for a week. And so Bobby's real knockout put an end to all of the fun just in time for everyone to return to school.

In the spring of the next year, my doctors told me I needed an operation and that I would have to spend the whole summer indoors. There would be no brilliant days but probably no more head injuries either, although I knew they would knock me out for the surgery. Summer came, school let out, I went to the hospital one evening, and in the morning, they put me on a cot and rolled me, covered only in a white sheet, into the operating room. The scars on my head from the summer before were now well hidden under a full head of hair. Maybe that's why the doctor went to so much trouble to explain to me how it would feel to be put under. He didn't know I was a pro. So after joking with me a bit in an effort to ease my nerves, he held the black mask over my face and told me to breathe deeply and evenly. I took a deep breath, and before I knew it, I was out.

Part 2: Father, Brother, Son

Dad and the Cops

When your father has a certain knack, it doesn't always mean you will have it. Sometimes you get it, sometimes you don't. My father had a knack for telling stories about himself. He liked to talk about his childhood and about the cops. I liked the stories, but I don't have the knack. When my children ask me to tell them about when I was little, I can never think of a thing to say. Instead, I retell my father's stories. The problem is that my kids don't know my father. He lost his mind from anger, old age, and pain, and they never heard him tell a story. He forgot himself and everything else, and then he died in an institution.

Dad had a thing about the cops. It seemed like he was always getting into trouble or expecting to get into trouble with them. But Dad never really had much of a run-in with the cops. Even at the end, when the cops picked him up, it was on a minor charge. But Dad always liked to talk about how the cops had it in for him. Once, he was arrested for talking back to an out-of-uniform cop. Dad was driving through the next town and a car pulled up alongside him at the arterial. The driver leaned an elbow out the car window and asked, "What's your name?"

"Schmidt! Who gives a shit?" Dad said.

The cop pinched him and told him to drive to city hall. The judge made him pay ten dollars for refusing to comply with the request of an officer.

"I tried to tell the judge that I didn't know he was a cop," Dad explained. "But the judge, he said, You should be more polite. That was an awful lot of money in those days."

I guess Dad's thing with the cops started with Officer Regan. He wasn't an officer really, at least not yet. He was a truck driver in the bag mill. He hauled rolls of papers, bags, big bearings, and sometimes wood chips back and forth between the loading docks and the guts of the paper mill where Dad and he worked. One time, as Dad told it, there was something of an industrial emergency. They needed a bearing ground to repair one of the giant paper machines. I think it was Number Three. Dad was the man for the job and he finished it in record time. Dad was always in a hurry. That's what makes this story so strange. After Dad finished, he was supposed to do what the foreman told him and grab the first truck driver who came along and send the bearing down to paper machine Number Three.

That's when Regan pulled his truck into the machine shop. He was a big, slow-moving man. He had big hands and big feet, and he never tucked in his shirt. When he was thinking, he used to run his big hand along the length of his head. He smoothed back his hair and settled his hand in a scratch on his neck. Then he stood there motionless, except for the big crablike hand crawling around on his neck.

Dad told Regan to run the bearing down to Number Three. But Regan didn't like to be told what to do, especially by a little runt. Dad wasn't so tall. In fact, he was an awful little guy. When the nurses in the home used to talk about him in later years, before he lost all sense of the world, they called him "that sweet little guy." But Dad wasn't so sweet. He just knew how to be polite. After talking so sweet to one of the nurses, he would give her the finger when she turned her back. But Dad was short, there was no contesting that.

In fact, when Dad was a kid, he was always getting into trouble because of his size. At least, that's what I think. Dad wasn't given to psychologizing. He just said what happened. A kid named Austin Wilkey decided he was going to pound the shit out of him. The problem was Austin couldn't punch his way out of a paper bag. And he lacked the confidence for the job. Personally, I think he picked Dad because he was the smallest guy he could find. He wanted to make something out of himself, but he didn't have the guts to make too much out of himself. He didn't have any friends, so he settled for an enemy, and he stuck with Dad because he was reliable and would do what had to be done. He told Dad they had to fight it out, and he waited for him every day at the bridge down by the upper mill.

"Porky," he'd say, "Today I can lick you."

"No you can't," Dad always said.

Then Dad would clean his clock.

The next day, Austin would be at the bridge again.

"Porky," he'd say, "Today I can lick you."

"No you can't," said Dad. And the same thing would happen.

The third time Mrs. Wilkey came over to the house to complain about Austin's ripped shirt. The old man asked Dad what the hell he thought he was about. "Dad," my father said, "he says he can lick me and he can't. What am I supposed to do?"

Then my grandfather punched Dad in the face and told him to stop fighting. Mrs. Wilkey went away satisfied. My grandfather wasn't the most understanding sort of man, but he did have a flair for politics and he loved a good contradiction. He used to take my Dad into the tavern, set him up on the bar, and give him a cigarette to smoke in front of all the guys.

"Look at the little shit smoke," he said, and all the men laughed. But later when he found Dad smoking on his own, he beat the crap out of him.

"That wasn't right," Dad used to say. "You can't teach a kid good habits that way."

Unfortunately for Dad, Austin was a persistent child, and the next day he was at the bridge, saying the same thing and getting the same thing done to him. Then Austin's mom had to go complain again, and Dad got punched in the mouth. It was beginning to look like Austin had found an indirect way of licking Dad. But he didn't know Dad. Dad was used to taking punches from the old man, and as long as Austin couldn't get in his own punches, he wasn't going to lick him. So, in the end, Austin gave out before Dad did. My grandfather stopped punching Dad for fighting with Austin and started punching him for doing something else.

Now, I suppose Regan scratched his neck for some time before he told Dad to go to hell.

"Go to hell," he said, "you're not my boss."

Dad just laughed. He must have been feeling mean that day because he didn't do a thing. Ordinarily, he would have taken that bearing down to the lower mill on his back because he was a man who believed in punctuality. But this time he sat down and had a cup of coffee. He sipped it real slow. Then he had another one.

Sure enough, the foreman came running into the shop. When

he saw Dad drinking coffee, he exploded. "Jesus Christ, what the hell are you doing?" he said. "Where's the goddamn bearing?"

"Right there," Dad said, pointing at the floor.

"Well, what the Christ is it doing there?" the foreman said.

"Well," Dad said, taking his time, "you told me to finish it up real fast, right? And then you told me to grab the first truck driver I saw and send it down to you, right? Well, that's what I did. But Regan here, he says I'm not his boss, and he won't do it. So, there she lies."

After Regan became a cop, he didn't forget about Dad. He'd arrest Dad for dropping a piece of paper on the street. In fact, once he did just that. It embarrassed the other cops down at the station and they let Dad go. But Regan didn't let go. He gave Dad an escort home every night. He used to lie in wait for him when he came out of the tavern or the mill and follow him home.

"His headlights were always in my ass," Dad used to say, "and I got damn sick of it. So, once, just to aggravate him, I decided to follow him around. I parked my car and sat until I saw him come by. Then I pulled out real slow and followed him around town. After a while, I guess he noticed me because he started to take turns. He sped up and I sped up. He slowed down and I slowed down. Then he stopped the police car and flagged me over."

"What you following me for?" Regan asked.

"I'm not following you," Dad said. "You keep going where I'm going."

Regan scratched his fat neck and then got back in his car and pulled away, and Dad got back in his car and followed him around town. But soon enough, he pulled over and flagged Dad again.

"You're following me," he said.

"What if I am?" Dad said, because he was pissed off. "It's a free country. Besides, you like driving around town with me. Every goddamn night you follow me home. You must like driving around town with me. I thought I'd save you the trouble."

Regan didn't have much to say to that. As Dad told it, he followed him around town for a bit longer and then went home. And Regan stopped following Dad, at least for a little while.

Regan didn't live too much longer, but Dad kept expecting

him to turn up around the next corner. Regan was the cop, lying in wait, parked behind the bushes in the entrance to St. Mary's cemetery. He was the cop who eased his car up tight against the savings and loan building and watched the stop sign on the corner for guys who liked to slip around it without coming to a full stop. At night when Dad drove past all the bright windows lined up on our street, Regan was the driver in the car just behind him. Sometimes having a car on his tail was enough to start Dad in on another Regan story.

Things got worse when my mother died. She died too slowly for anyone to be able to take it. First she lost an eye, and they got her an artificial one. Then she got ovarian cancer. She began to dry up, and the plastic eye wouldn't fit in her eye socket anymore. It kept popping out. She finally gave up putting it in altogether, even though she was a woman who was proud of her appearance. The eye got infected, and Dad worked on it every night. He bathed the eye patch in warm water until he could remove the tape without causing too much pain. Night after night, until she had no eyebrow left, he pulled away the tape and a few hairs with it. Then he used a Q-tip to swab the pus out of the socket. He tried to keep a straight face during the job. But the eye smelled pretty bad, and it was a heartbreaking job. "Christ," he said, "it stinks." Toward the end, when Mom finally went into the hospital for good, the nurses wouldn't even do the job—not that Dad would have let them.

After Mom died, Dad stopped doing everything. He was more or less finished. He tried to recover but nothing worked. He pasted a picture of Mom on the dashboard of his Buick so he could see her while he was driving around town. It was a nice picture. It looked like it was taken on the day of my sister's wedding because Mom was in a formal dress. She sat on the couch in the living room with her head tilting ever so slightly to the right. She looked pretty contented. But Dad was nervous for the first time. He talked a lot about being extra careful so the cops wouldn't take the car away from him.

"I never drink when I'm going to drive," he'd say on the phone.

"They won't catch me with a drink on my breath and take away my car. If I think I'm going to drive, I don't touch anything."

The fact that he was talking about not drinking and driving should have told me that he probably was. But it was hard for us kids to think Dad was turning into a drunk. Most of the time, he seemed to be in pretty good shape. Other times, he didn't make much sense. We thought he was getting old.

Then, one hot summer night, I got a long-distance call from the cops. It wasn't clear what had happened. Dad was in a car accident. Then it turned out that the other vehicle was a motorbike. The kid on the motorbike wasn't hurt, which was amazing, considering the size of a Buick. Maybe this was one lucky kid. But Dad didn't even hit anyone. He ran over a motorbike parked in front of the Ideal Cafe three times before a cop knocked on his car window and drew his attention to the fact that he was dragging the bike back and forth under the Buick.

The cops tried to give Dad a breathalyzer test, but he couldn't blow into the machine. Then they took him into the emergency room and gave him a blood test. He was drunk, but since the blood test wouldn't be filed for forty-eight hours, the cops couldn't arrest him. They left his car parked downtown in front of the Ideal, drove him home, and told him to go to bed. But Dad never did what the cops told him to do. A neighbor boy who cut Dad's lawn heard a commotion and went over to the house to check it out. He found Dad in the garage covered with sweat. He was rummaging through a lumber pile with a flashlight. There were garbage cans and tools all over the back yard, and Dad's snowblower was parked on the front lawn. When the kid asked him what he was doing, Dad told him he was looking for his car.

After that I put Dad in a nursing home. The doctor found evidence of two strokes, and it was clear that Dad couldn't live alone anymore. He didn't know why he was there or where he was. He blamed it on the cops. As he told it, he was leaving the Ideal Cafe when some guy gave him a paper cup half full of coffee.

"It was full of old coffee," he said, "so I tried to dump it at the curb in front of the Ideal. But I dropped the cup, and that cop, he was right there to pinch me."

I let Dad go on believing the story because I didn't know what to say when he asked me when he could go home. I told him his own cop story, and he just nodded, and then said, "It's just not right. All you have to do is slip up once."

But Dad wouldn't stay put. He went through the door of the home "on the average of six times every half an hour," the head nurse said. The nurses said he was a sweet old guy. The called him Houdini II. But they got tired of him pretty fast. They gave him Thorazine to take the edge off. Then he only went through the door once or twice a day. On average.

One day a nurse thought she'd do him a favor and take him for a walk. She walked him twice around the building and then tried to get him back inside. He told her he had to go take care of his sick wife and started for town. The nurse tried to grab him and he threw a punch at her. He missed but it was close enough for her. She called the cops to come pick him up. This is Dad's last cop story. The police car pulled up beside him as he was hotfooting it home. The driver rolled down the window, leaned out an elbow, and asked Dad his name.

Better Son Than Father

I have been a better son than a father. That is what I am—a son. It explains a lot about my personality. I am a bad father because I expect other people to be responsible and mature—in the case of my children, before they are able to bear this kind of responsibility. I am myself obedient. I know how to follow orders and how to behave myself. I know how to pitch in when I am asked. I have a hard time refusing money when it is offered because it is the father's right to pay and I am a son. My father always paid, and I felt like I was compromising him whenever I tried to pay the bill. I feel the same way about other people, whether they are older or younger, men or women. If they pay, I feel it is my duty to accept graciously. A friend of mine has the habit of holding doors for other people. I always feel awkward having him hold a door for me, but I feel more awkward not having him hold it because I know he thinks of it as a kindness.

When my parents became sick and old, I felt it was my duty to be their son, to take care of them, even though I have three siblings. My father once told me on a visit to see my dying mother that I was a good son. It was the only time he ever said it to me. He said it not like he was surprised that I was a good son but like he was surprised to hear himself say it—surprised because the words were a way of talking about his parting from my mother, as if my being a good son was tied to her dying and reminded him of it.

I have good children. They are loving and intelligent and considerate. But I am afraid they will grow up thinking they are not good enough because no matter how good they are, my message to them seems to be that they could be better. I give them a dose of reproachfulness in every act and word. I remember my father telling me that I shouldn't get married, and if I did, I shouldn't have children. I took him to be saying that both are a sadness to a man. He didn't want me to take it the wrong way. He told me he loved his children, but he said they weighed down your life. He actually took my brother and his wife aside and gave them the same advice, and they took it to heart.

I could never have made the choice my brother made—not to have children—because I am first of all my father's son, and one of a son's duties is to bring other sons into the world, sons of the father's sons. And so I have a daughter and a son. I see my father in my son. I hope he grows up to be a better father than I have been. It is good to be a father.

Four Men, Four Walls, and a Fire

For a brief period in the life of men, when they go off to school or to seek their fortune, they live together in small households. It is one of the most unnatural situations a man will ever experience, but at the time it seems completely natural. Two men may live together happily if one has been well brought up by his mother. When more than two men set up a household together, they automatically forget everything their mothers taught them.

The rooms become a pigsty. Dust blossoms in the highlands. Magazines, half-empty bottles, potato chips, tennis shoes and socks, pizza boxes, and hairballs collect in the lowlands. The rug in the bathroom needs to be thrown away but never is. Bizarre tribal behavior takes the place of politeness and manners. The fork is set to the right of the plate, if eating implements are used at all. Impolite greetings involving body fluids, domestic animals, and a man's mother are shouted out with regularity. Cooking does not disappear, but that which goes by the name of cooking usually does. Experimental science is a better name to describe what men do with food.

For a short time in my life, I lived in three of these households. One stands out in my memory because it had the usual strangeness of the male household in the extreme. The household was also memorable because my brother was one of my roommates, and it was the first time I had ever lived with him away from home. There were two other men in the apartment. One was my friend Al; the other was my brother's friend Ray. Both were innocents. An innocent is a man who seems to be asleep at the wheel yet gets where he's going just the same. He usually suffers from either peerless single-mindedness or reckless abandon. Al was the single-minded one. He studied all the time. Being acutely aware of the physics of the grease molecules in his scalp, he would wash his hair at any hour of the day or night. Ray was a lover of heavy-metal music. He would sit for hours listening to it through headphones with an expression on his face that made you think of Mozart. He owned a bathrobe and wore it, sometimes for days on end. He also practiced knife-throwing with our butcher knife, hurling it into the panels of oak doors. When any of us reached for a doorknob we shouted, "Put the knife down, Ray!"

The behavior of an innocent always seems completely natural to him because he never does anything except for the reason that he wants to do it. He has no hidden motives and he is not anxious to please other people. In fact, he usually acts as if other people don't exist at all. He doesn't appear to be interested in sex, although he thinks about women all the time. Above all, an innocent should not be living with other men. Eventually, he realizes it and winds up getting a place by himself or with a woman.

Calling a man an innocent is no insult. All men tend toward innocence. Living with other men only brings out the extreme cases. It may be objected that their behavior is inconsiderate and rebellious, but men in this condition aren't being impolite. And they are too innocent to rebel against anything.

Our building was a three-story with a flat on each floor. We were sandwiched in the middle. Above us was a very unsuccessful five-man rock and roll band. They spent all of their time listening to loud music. They smoked a lot of dope, and they all played the same instrument—air guitar. Their sessions ended late every night when we bounced a basketball up against the ceiling of our apartment for more than ten minutes in a row.

Below us was a couple living together. She was . . . she was the only woman in the building. She had brown hair and she was pretty. Occasionally, I would run into her in the basement laundry. It was always an unnerving experience to be alone with the only woman in a house of ten men.

Her boyfriend was the manager of the property. He was a little guy with glasses who knew a lot about building mechanics—fuse boxes, plumbing, furnaces. He also seemed to know a lot about women as he was living with one. He had what I thought was a raunchy side to him, too. Once he asked me to water their plants. Their apartment looked like a real apartment—it actually had plants. It also had rugs, furniture, and pictures on the walls. But there was a touch of black velvet in the air, a red light bulb in the bedroom, and a copy of *The Joy of Sex* on the bedside table.

The owner of the building was an alcoholic. When he came for a visit, it always followed the same pattern. He knocked at the door, we opened it, and he made a beeline, without a greeting, to the refrigerator, where he helped himself to a beer. As ours was a house of men he was never disappointed. He got the beer out, opened it, and took a tall drink. Only then did he tell us his business. He was a great talker, and once he got started, he would stay for hours, plundering our supplies. He was forty-five and always dressed in a dark brown hunting outfit. He looked like a brown-haired Papa Hemingway without a shotgun.

The night of the fire, I was shut up in my room, even though it was a beautiful spring evening. I smelled smoke. My eye was drawn to a trap door in the floor that sealed off an old air shaft. Smoke was wafting up out of it. My gut reaction was to throw open the trap. But I ran out into the living room and called out to my brother and Ray instead. Ray phoned the fire department. I went upstairs to clear out the third floor, and my brother ran down the rear stairs to warn the couple below us. He found her alone in the apartment, asleep in a room directly over the fire. The smoke smelled strong. She was groggy, but he got her up and out of the building.

Everyone gathered at the side of the building on the main street, waiting for the firemen to arrive. Everyone except Ray. Two big fire trucks rolled up the street and pulled in next to the building. The firemen jumped off their trucks and in no time were inside, securing the basement and the three upper floors. Other firemen stood around the trucks with us, asking questions about the building and the call.

Suddenly Ray appeared on the second-floor balcony. He had wrapped his head and body in his blue bedspread and was cradling something in his arms. He looked like a cross between Barbra Streisand during her Afro phase and the Virgin Mary. He was jumping around and yelling out in a falsetto, "My baby! My baby! Save my baby!" Then he flung the bundle off the balcony. Two firemen dived for it as it fell past us. They crashed into each other, missed the catch, and the bundle hit the ground without a bounce or a cry. It was a pillow wrapped up in a bath towel. The firemen were not at all happy. From the look on their faces, I thought they were going to pack up and leave. But they stayed to put out the fire anyway, more out of civic duty than personal charity. Afterward, one of them told me that the house would have gone up like a match if I had opened the trap door, that it had not been closed off at the bottom according to code. He also told me to get rid of the roommate.

This was not the last time Ray got himself into trouble. Not long afterward he was arrested when a driver for the Madison Mass Transit Company called him in. The cops found him in the back of the bus in a loving embrace, like some drunken Pygmalion, with a life-size plastic Venus de Milo. He had snatched her from a florist shop downtown, but he was too drunk to escort her home. So he caught a city bus, lifted his lady love over the threshold, gallantly paid her passage, and then conducted her to the rear seat for the ride home. He called us from jail the next morning, when he remembered his phone number, and my brother went downtown and bailed him out.

Our landlord was so happy we saved his building that he decided to throw a party for the whole house. Two weeks later, unannounced and on a Wednesday night, he arrived at our front door with a half-barrel of beer. He hauled the metal keg into the bathroom, put it on ice in the tub, and clamored up and down the stairs, inviting everyone to his party. Three of the third-floor band members were at home and glad to be diverted for the evening. The building manager had a polite one or two drinks and left for home.

We, of course, had nowhere to go. My brother and Ray grabbed a few comfortable chairs and some good glasses and dug in for the duration. I had an inspiration after three beers and called my girlfriend to bail me out. Al left in a hurry for the library, complaining about his upcoming exams. In fact, he was on the wagon with a vengeance. A few weeks before, he had returned late from the library to one of our parties and made the mistake of drinking some of my punch, even though its maker was drinking beer. Then he made another mistake and belittled women's physical strength to my girlfriend, who promptly challenged him to a foot race around the block. He beat her by a neck, barely saving his pride, but the combination of night air, exertion, and punch went right to his head, and he collapsed into bed. Later that night I heard strange coughs coming from his room and found him throwing up into his pillow. I dragged him into the bathroom and bent him over the toilet. When he was better than empty, I cleaned him up, stripped the sheets off his bed, and threw him back into it. He awoke without a memory of the night before but with the firm resolve to avoid parties.

When I returned home the next morning, our landlord was gone, two band members were passed out in a heap on the living-room floor, and I had the pleasure of showering with the silvery keg. It was still at least half full, and the beer was as warm as breast milk. Two more days passed before the landlord relieved me of its companionship.

The fire is my only experience to date with a house fire, and it was not much of a fire, if one can say that about any fire in a house. Still, I am tempted to describe it that way, and when I think about it, I realize my attitude is left over from the general mood of those times when I lived in the company of men. We saw any happening, no matter how serious, either as having no consequence or as an occasion for merriment. According to the general measure of things, this meant that the most serious moments in our lives inspired only comedy and that day to day we were doing little more than playing. Our play was a form of forgetting and a form of becoming. We were actively forgetting who we had been in order to become who we now are, and we were having a lot of fun in the process.

The best thing about the household was that I learned who my brother was for the first time. At times we were inseparable, and the old hierarchy between older and younger disappeared between us. On one occasion, we decided to drive home to see our parents for the weekend. We started out on the three-hour drive much too late in the evening and in the worst of weather. It was dead winter, and a life warning had been issued. A life warning is an alert in cold weather that defines conditions as so life-threatening that a man can't expect to survive the cold long enough to make his way even a short distance by foot. Every year in that part of the country a few people freeze to death because they try to cross a small field to reach the lights of a farmhouse. The car we were driving was the family wreck, loaned to us in perpetuity by our father. For some reason, no doubt scenic, we had decided not to take the interstate highway but the back roads. The car stalled every few miles. When we got out to look under the hood, the cold radiated in a flash from the pavement up through the soles of our shoes to our knees. We had to douse the carburetor with alcohol to restart the engine each time it quit. Eventually we figured out that it would not stall if we held our speed to twenty miles per hour.

So we began the long crawl home, and because it was going to take so long we didn't care about the time. We also got very hungry. We stopped at a small pizza place, leaving the car running in the parking lot, the key in the ignition and the doors unlocked, and settled in for a pizza or two and some pitchers of beer. We stayed hours, talking about our father and mother and family, before getting back on the road. When we finally arrived home, we found our parents sitting in the dark by the door, paralyzed with worry, bent into the frozen shapes in which they expected the county police would discover us. It had never occurred to us to call them, even though they were waiting for us and we had spent most of the night reminiscing about them.

I thought I had been playing with my brother all my life and I thought I knew who he was. But in our first household of men I learned how to play anew and differently with him, and in the high seriousness of our antics, I came to know him as a man—which was a lucky thing, because he was then putting aside his boyhood to become a man and a man he has continued to be.

The household disbanded that spring soon after the fire when the landlord sold the property to three or four lawyers. They made up quite a pack, acting and dressing alike. They came over once to interview us, saying they wanted responsible tenants, and once more to give congratulations when they decided to rent to us. They would need to ask for more money, however. We made the case that they should not raise our rent since we were such responsible tenants and responsible tenants were hard to find. We threatened to move if they didn't back down. They didn't, and we kept our word.

The apartment had brought us together, and when we left it, things changed. Ray quit school. The last time I saw him he was standing on top of a four-story silo. No one I know has seen or heard of him since. Al got a studio apartment by himself. I see him every few years by accident. My brother and I stuck together to make up the heart of another male household. We now live thousands of miles apart and have very different lives, but whenever I talk to him, I know we are still members of the same house of men.

My Mother's Red Shoe

No one knows I wear my mother's red shoe.

Several of my father's ties have come down to me. One he wore at my sister's wedding. It is black, medium gray, and silver. When I wear it, it gives me a pleasantly antiquated look, or so I imagine. In my mind's eye, the tie hangs around my father's neck, and I wear my father's tie.

With it I wear my mother's red shoe.

I have a pin given to my father for working at the same company for thirty years. It is a rectangular gold pin with a diamond chip in a size reserved for attestations of service to men who are important but not too important. The company name is written on the pin. I use it to affect a bit of style, sometimes attaching it to my collar in place of a tie.

No one ever notices the name of the company, but the name will be forever associated in my mind with my father and my life in his house. The company was a paper mill, and it gave off a strong and bitter smell that soaked into his skin and clothes and belongings. He also left me a fine box of professional tools lined with green felt that I keep locked tightly to this day. Whenever I open it, the aroma of the mill tries to escape. I keep the box closed to trap the smell for a million years.

Once I bought two pairs of maroon oxford shoes with tassels. My right foot is shriveled from polio, so I bought a man's pair for my left foot and a matching woman's pair for my right. I took the left shoe from the man's pair and the right shoe from the woman's pair and threw away the odd set. But the right shoe was too tight because I had no experience buying women's shoes. Then my mother died, and I had to clean out her closet. There I found a pair of maroon oxford shoes with tassels. They were a larger size than mine and nicely broken in. I put on the right shoe. It felt good and matched my other one. I remembered with a smile that my mother had a thing for red shoes. This is as close as I can get, I thought. I kept her right shoe and threw away the odd set.

No one knows I wear my mother's red shoe.

Harold Siebers, 1915–1994

All depends upon whether one is willing to labor and be heavy laden. —KIERKEGAARD

We are all unremarkable people, I suppose. We are born, live, and die. None of us here is a captain of industry, a president, or a poet. But we all have something remarkable about our unremarkableness.

It is sometimes hard for me to remember what was remarkable about my father because in his last years he lost his reason and forgot who he was. It tempted me as well to forget who he was.

My father was remarkable for three things. They were simple things but not simple to accomplish.

First, he never gave up, no matter what. He had a third-grade education, but he never closed his mind and he was always on the move. He was a mechanical genius, but his true genius lay in his absolute refusal to drop what he had started. When he took on a job, a hard job, he quit only when it was done. And he did it right.

Second, my father knew how to work. Work was all-important to him. He didn't do it because he liked it. He worked because things needed to be done. When he worked, he worked harder and longer than anyone I ever saw.

Last, my father told stories about his life, and by doing so, he made his unremarkable life seem remarkable, and those who heard his stories thought that maybe their lives were remarkable, too. We all need someone in our life who knows who he is, because that helps us to know who we are. My father knew who he was.

A man can count on two good things if he is lucky and lives well as a man: that he will have been faithful at death to his beliefs and that he will die as himself. I am sorry that my father forgot at the end of his life who he was. But all of us here know who he was. I know who my father was, and I will never forget him.

April 11, 1994

Packing Up the Tool Box

I have something on my hands. I can't get rid of it. It's not grease or simple dirt. It smells of iron, sweat, rust, and a little blood. The kind that flows from broken knuckles. My hands smell of it. It won't go away if I don't let it.

Tools sweat when they work. Like people. When they get old, they outgrow their usefulness. Like people. They lie about in a clutter, smelling like old tools, behaving like old tools. Like people.

Tools are made of iron and wood. There are 11 wrenches, 3 hammers (1 claw, 2 ball peen), 9 screwdrivers, 6 metal punches, 18 files, 4 jackknives, 4 saw blades, 1 cyclometer, 7 calipers, 2 pencil erasers, 2 cigarette lighters, 1 bottle, 2 soldering irons, 1 T square, 5 chucks, 1 crowbar, 2 planes, 7 tape measures, 3 sets of socket wrenches (2 regular, 1 metric), 13 pencil stubs, 1 cigarette butt (Salem filter), 2 rolls of electric tape, 3 levels, 1 nail clipper, 1 pair of leather gloves, 1 nail puller, 32 drills (iron and wood), 5 golf tees.

Everything is a tool. Tools of the trade. Hand tools. Electric tools. Professional tools. In boxes as old as the tools.

Each tool recalls the hands that worked it. Each speck of dirt, each metal filing, each scrap of paper, each piece of wire, each nut, each broken bolt, each twisted nail has been kept to fulfill its purpose, if only to be kept to no purpose.

I have something on my hands. I have to pack up my father's tools. Let us be sure that we have them all. There are too many to count. It's a matter of intuition. None must escape. Nothing must be thrown away. Nothing must change in the tool box.

Pictures of My Father

Now that my father has died, I find myself thinking more and more about my mother. It is as if part of my mourning for him is a renewed mourning for her, or that in mourning my father, I feel the loss of both of them. The focus of my feelings is a photograph of them in a small round brass frame. It was one of the photographs my father framed after my mother died. He kept a few photographs of my mother, by herself or with him, on the desk in the dining room. They seemed at the time to be almost clutter. The choice of photographs was strange, and the frames were cheap—the kind you get from a bank for opening a checking account.

Nevertheless, when I sold my father's house, I put them all in the box that I planned to keep for the family to go through upon his death. I left the box at my sister's house in Wisconsin. When Dad died, I went back there to his funeral. One day before we all looked through the box together, I went through it alone, and when I saw this photograph I wanted it. I was afraid someone else would want it, too, so I took it out of the box on the sly and kept it. Then, instead of mailing it to my house in Michigan with the other things that fell to me the next day when I sat with my brother and sisters over the box, I carried it with me in my pocket on the plane. I put it on my bedside table.

This photograph is one of the first things I see in the morning and one of the last at night. I look at it many times each day because I come into the room to get some change from the bowl next to it, or take off my watch and put it there on the table, or take a nap and remove my glasses and set them next to the photo. I have a place for all these things. Now the photograph of my parents has found its place among them at the center of my life, and I visit it as if it were a shrine.

It is a beautiful picture of my mother. Her face is open and she is staring directly into my eyes. She is smiling slightly, like the Mona Lisa, and on her lips is her favorite dark red lipstick. Her hair is done up. She is wearing her cream cashmere sweater buttoned to the neck without a blouse underneath. I can't tell how old she is, maybe forty-eight or fifty. It is the age when I remember her best, the age when I recognize her as my mother.

My father sits to her left, their arms overlapping; they are sitting so close together. He is wearing a white short-sleeved shirt, so it must be early fall or spring. I can see his white T-shirt at his collar. His eyes are smiling and squinting in his manner—they look almost closed, but the eyebrows are arched, so you know they are open. His mouth is downturned slightly, but he is wearing a smile because his upper lip is drawn up and not pushing down. He is not wearing glasses.

Most of the time as he grew older, my father wore his glasses, but sometimes he just took them off, and he could still see. It always surprised me. I always thought of glasses as part of a person's anatomy, and I think of them that way now, since I have begun to wear them and never think of taking them off if I want to see anything. But glasses were more in the category of tools for my father. He used them to do certain things. I remember in the old-age home at the end, he used to hide or break his glasses, and we finally gave up supplying him with them. It didn't seem to matter. All of a sudden he could see without them. One time he picked me out at the length of a long hall, even though he hadn't seen me in more than six months and didn't know who he was himself.

In the photograph he has set aside his glasses. He is looking directly into my face as well—my mother and father looking at me. I see two beloved people, my mother and father, my friends—people who loved me without question and whom I loved without fault. I know now why my father picked out this picture to look at every day.

The Metaphysics of Lawn Care

What do you do when your parents are dead and your lawn won't grow in the right direction?

You may talk to your children about it, but they understand only that the mud on their shoes should not be tracked in where the people live. You may consult your good wife, and in wifely duties find a house of hope beyond the attractions, dead gravities, and sinister tangles of plant life, but the fact remains that carpets obey a duller metaphysics than the lawn and no amount of hope inside will fatten the grass to a brilliant green.

The compass is as necessary to a good lawn as to a good life. The hemisphere matters, and the direction of the blade, like the flow of the waters, differs from north to south. If your lawn is directionless, if the hemispheres are out of kilter, if the waters flow up instead of down, what chance do you have to perfect yourself and to make of your image—fatherless, motherless—a geography likened to the world's?

The lawn has its own sense in the minor world of ants and aphids, but as the keeper of the grasses in the world above, the one who charts the direction of the stars beyond and of vegetable love below, it is for you to decide whether to set your blade to the same old metaphysics or to cut against the grain of your own hemisphere.

Part 3: Love and Lust

The Fate of Marriage

They were so poor they could afford only to drive down from the Fox River Valley to the Milwaukee Zoo for the pleasure of making a honeymoon. In later years, their idea of happiness would be to drive somewhere, up to Sault Sainte Marie and across the Mackinaw Bridge into lower Michigan, where they would buy their children tiny wooden shoes with their names burned into them with a hot pen, then down and around to Chicago and back up to the heart of the valley, completing a circle around Lake Michigan.

The honeymoon hotel must have been what they called in those days a "dive," but it was at least in the big city. It was July 16, 1938. The room was stifling, and after they made love for the first time as husband and wife, he moved out of the bed and laid himself out on the cool linoleum floor. At the zoo they saw the animals. The next day he was back at work in the sour air of the mill, fixing the machines that make paper. Nine months later she gave birth to a baby girl, my eldest sister sweet Linda, and they became "mother and father," just as they had become, like a thousand generations before them, "husband and wife."

Marriage is a bargain where two people exchange names for the sake of happiness. Each one promises to be someone for the other, a "husband" or "wife," and to respond when the name is called. And yet husbands and wives are always more or less than these words imply. Usually more, even when they are less—especially when they are less. The couple in a good marriage understands what is true in marriage good or bad: we are most human when we fail to live up to our promises. And so marriage is a bargain based on the inability of husband and wife, from time to time, with the best of intentions, to live up to the bargain. This is the truth of marriage—that love may grow deeper through disappointment.

In an age when even the mention of "husband and wife" is likely to give offense, what is the fate of marriage? I can't say. Like all married people, I only know what marriage should be, not what it is or what will become of it. It is one of the many absurdities of the wedded state that everyone knows what it should be and no one knows what it is. A million stories exist to describe it for you and to make your own efforts seem crippled or shopworn by comparison. The stories of other people's marriages can be either divine or wretched, but they are always completely different from the story of your own. Marriage is for this reason a miracle of plenty from penury, a miracle that requires a leap of faith across the chasm between man and woman, between anarchy and conviction, on the wings of a few flimsy words. "Husband and wife." "Father and mother." "You and me." "We." The extremes of daydream and night terror meet as lovers and take to bed: pleasure and pain, home and hunt, friendship and lust, heaven and earth. Marriages are made in heaven, but they make their living far below, in a world where faith is unmade, and they feel the strain at every earthly moment.

The fate of marriage is most obviously embodied in the flesh of man and woman. They are undoubtedly twins, like the two sides of Plato's cuttlefish sliced in two by God and forever yearning to be reunited with their better halves. And yet the individual desires of twins, however identical, have their own timing, and men and women seem forever cursed to suffer from bad timing—when the man turns left, the woman turns right. This alone would be reason to bring marriage to ruin, but it also provides a good enough reason to make the attempt: the degree of difficulty of the union is not without its challenge. Man and woman clasp one another in momentary bliss, like two trapeze artists who somersault into an embrace without a net, and then swing back to their respective extremes.

Perhaps it is the difficulty of marriage that condemns it to embody so many of life's contradictions. It is one of our finest ideals of happiness and one of our deepest sources of suffering. It may be for our kind the only place where true happiness is to be found, and yet this happiness seems a cruel sham to those who have never had it and a small wonder to those who have. All that need happen for two people to find love is to ask it of each other. Love is all we want. We can have it all the time, and we don't ask for it. And no one knows why not.

For generations, men have been the prime movers in matters of love. They were responsible for its timing and bore the blame when the timing was bad. (In sex they still do.) Men are creatures of desire, and women have been assured of this desire because it is directed toward them with a violence that can't be ignored and obviously takes a huge toll. The rhetoric of masculinity and femininity, of activity and passivity, was forged during a millennium of coupling, and it is still very much a habitual part of erotic life. To desire and to be desired are actions that can't exist independently, and yet these verbs are separated by an abyss, and it has been men's storied task to traverse it.

Now a new age of sexuality has dawned—women may name their own desire instead of having it named by men. This is a good thing, but I think women will soon find out what men have long known: the initiator is never sure desire will be returned. Sex exposed attracts more sex, as surely as honey brings houseflies. People have sex, even if they don't like it very much, and they will usually accept it when it is offered. Otherwise, men would not take to bed without feeling, and women would not wake up in the morning wishing they hadn't. The problem is that men and women, though their attractions may begin in sex, want them to end in love, and love is a more perplexing form of companionship than sex because you always know when you are having sex but you rarely know for sure if you are being loved.

Men experience sexual compulsion very early in life. They know how lust can overwhelm and humiliate them, and so they fear its effects on themselves and on the women they love. Plutarch wrote in his essays on marriage that a wife should not be offended if her husband takes his desire to a whore because it shows he honors her as a wife. The idea has no value at all except to suggest that men have always been afraid that their desire will harm or debase their wives. As far as I know, women have not yet begun to worry that their desires might debase their husbands, and there probably won't be anything like true sexual equality until they do. For men, however, the idea remains as powerful now as it was for Plutarch, and they feel the terror of their desire at every moment. Today, women are more likely than men to charge that male desire is violent, to maintain that all forms of sexual intercourse with men are harmful to women. If this is right, then men's worst fears have been realized—they will never be able to escape the terror and truth of their own desire—and they are the sadder sex. What could be worse than to know your love hurts the one you love? Unless it be to know love only as accepting to be hurt? In which case women are the sadder sex.

I might have made a life with any one of the women I have loved. I was usually ready to marry them at any given moment, but they were not eager for marriage—at least that is what I told myself at the time. Actually, they were not eager to marry me. They all did marry someone else, and soon enough after we broke up for the decision not to have reflected a change of attitude, only a better choice. When I did find someone who wanted to marry me as much as I did her, it seemed wise to ask her and to behave myself around her, out of gratitude as much as love. This sounds rather casual for a romance. It wasn't and isn't.

My own marriage was decided because I was about to go off to France for a year. It is a strange truth that marriage is often decided by external circumstances, even though its moving force comes from inside of us. Jill had just been involved with a young man who had gone off to England. They had agreed to remain true to each other, but they could date whomever they wanted in the interim—freedom being more the rage at the time than faithfulness. I became the whoever, and he came back ancient history, though not without value as a history lesson: fidelity works better in theory than in practice, so if you want it, you had better practice it. On my way to a country more romantic than England, I was not about to repeat his mistake. I asked Jill to marry me before I left for France. She arranged to graduate from college in December, a semester early, and join me in Paris for the rest of the year. I was to cash in the student loans I had been squirreling away for a start in life in order to keep a roof over our heads and to put an occasional pastry on a table for two.

It was 1978, the time of the Equal Rights Amendment, to give something of the flavor of the epoch. Jill had marched on Washington with women friends that summer and called herself a feminist. I left for Paris and soon became friendly with an older woman, an American college professor, who became my confidante and advisor. She was a lesbian and, I supposed, knew everything about making women happy, being one herself and spending all her time with them. She became my conscience in matters of sexual honor, because at that time I saw lesbianism as the superego of the women's movement. I only abandoned this view years later, after going to the public lecture of a famous feminist. The lecture was a stand-up comedy routine in the style of Henny Youngman, only the punch line had changed to "Take my husband... Please!" The women in the audience were howling with laughter, and some of the men were, too. The rest took the safe, stoic approach and sat very still. So this was equality, I thought, the equal right to ridicule. Actually, when I look back on it, the lecture was pretty funny, and I was too hard on the speaker and her audience. Any joking on this subject is welcome, and the more of it, the better. But the experience did shake my confidence in feminism and make me realize that no movement will ever offer a solution to the heartaches of men and women. Only particular men and women find something that works for them, and even these solutions look good only from the safe distance of two score and ten years, when old, toothless, and a little blind, husband and wife glance back on their wedded life together with a sense of nostalgia and well-deserved satisfaction.

But back to 1978. My lesbian conscience was worried about Jill and me because I had made the perhaps irreparable mistake of having promised to cash in my student loans to buy our happiness. Money had been messing up love since time immemorial, she explained to me, and it was one of the many ways by which men controlled women—another being the offering of food in exchange for sex. My conscience told me it would be far better if Jill asked her mother for the money to live in Paris, because it was a way of subverting patriarchy and strengthening an alternative maternal bond. Apparently, it was still all right for Jill and me to go out to dinner on occasion, since I was feeding my conscience on a regular basis, and I remember she took me out one night to Au Pied de Cochon for a bite of their famed onion soup.

Between man and woman, however, the exchange of money was strictly forbidden.

My concern was sincere when I wrote Jill the letter with the idea that she go to her mother for money. Jill rightly saw it as a breach of my promise and thought I might be trying to squirm out of our relationship in the bargain, since she had no money of her own to make the trip and had agreed to use mine, even though she thought it was a bad idea. It took a considerable amount of mending, with little help from the French postal system, to get matters back to square one and Jill to Paris that December. So I stopped seeing my conscience and asking her advice and tried to listen to what Jill was telling me about what she wanted and what felt right to her. I guess I should have realized that my conscience's track record didn't speak too highly for her advice. She had been married herself to a sensitive and kindly man, from what I could tell about him. He had followed her around the country, leaving one good job after another, before she found her present teaching post. He had accepted her new erotic life when she declared she was a lesbian, and he had been known to bake cookies for lesbian lovers who came to tea. When he finally had a belly full of cookies and his wife's lovers, they divorced.

I am told men and women in a marriage undergo what is to all appearances a pattern of addiction to two different drugs. The first four years are a constant high on phenylethylamine, a natural amphetamine produced by the body: couples make love all night long, race from entertainment to entertainment, and throw plates when they fight. Eventually, though, their nerve endings wear down, and so must some of the giddiness. Then the chemistry of love begins to manufacture endorphins, a narcotic like opium that has a relaxing and calming effect—the perfect condiment for intimate talk and cozy evenings at home. Divorce usually occurs when a couple is switching from the first drug to the second, because the timing is delicate and drug addiction is volatile. The seven-year itch is really a fourth-year famine as couples begin to crave more speed to increase the intensity of their decaying passion. If they survive withdrawal, they become more attached to each other and acquire a taste for the mellow pleasure of endorphins. Those whose taste for speed will not die keep switching partners until they burn out. Then they either live alone or settle down happily with whomever they happen to be living at the time, whether a soul mate or not. This explains the strange bedfellows made by some third and fourth marriages.

An endorphin addict now for many years, I am beginning to fear divorce less and less, although there are still days when it seems inevitable. The hardest thing in my married life has not been remaining at home, controlling my lust for other women, or harming Jill with my desire, though I continue to be fearful of the last. My lust—that is, the aspects I can talk about with modesty—is remarkably single-minded, and I have not usually felt more than vague erotic interest in other women. Only once in my married years have I felt a strong attraction for another woman, and it was ultimately of the most transient kind. A young woman appeared from time to time in the corridors and streets I frequent. The first time I saw her I felt a sexual thrill shoot through my veins. I had only had this experience once before, with marriage as the consequence, and since it seemed to repeat itself every time I turned a corner and found myself face to face with her, I reasonably ascribed the effect to her and worried what I should do about it.

Luckily I did nothing. As time passed, I decided that this sexual rush belonged to a new phase in the chemistry of my body: it kept returning in different forms and different connections to the point of being almost commonplace, like a postmenstrual hot flash. It can't be called trivial because it is too intense, but it is by now familiar enough that I try not to confuse its appearance with any particular cause. I tell myself that the young brown-eyed woman with the firm breast and bouffant hairdo neatly blanketed in a scarf who sits before me in the subway, staring into her compact, her lips pursed to receive a deep red lipstick, is merely the occasion for and not the cause of the lust rising in my blood.

I need not run off with the tall blonde woman with the crew cut in the supermarket because I like her thin hands, long fingers, man's silver watch, and the way she keeps touching and arranging her oranges and yogurt at the checkout counter. No, these lovely women don't generate the sexual heat I feel—it comes from inside of me. My system is like a rocket jettisoning its third stage, purging itself of the dead freight of unneeded sexual fuel before I accept the causal orbit of old age where only the momentum of life and not its inner vitality keeps one in motion. Or maybe this is too macho an image. My occasional case of sexual vapors is more like the steam rising off a well-cooked egg as it begins to cool.

The hardest thing in married life for me has been keeping my mouth shut, and if Jill ever divorces me, that will be the cause. I am a small inventor of advice, offering her a dozen contraptions every day. Since every now and then my advice makes sense and because she loves me well, she is obliged to inspect my little inventions with wonder and appreciation, and listen to the small noises they make. But my advice is erratic, to use the kindest word available, and I really don't know what's best for her. Add to this the fact that I get hurt or angry too easily and am prone to say "I told you so," and you have the perfect recipe for quarrels. But nothing so serious to do anything about, so I end by causing a thousand exasperations every day.

I resolve to keep quiet in general, to console rather than advise. In particular, I resolve where high explosives are involved not to say the smallest word, not to provide the tiniest spark. It is usually forty-five seconds after my resolution has jelled to its firmest that I run off at the mouth. As I launch opinion after opinion, racing toward disaster, my mind tries to get the attention of whatever has taken control of my mouth. The result is usually a swerve or two in the argument but no general change in direction and, certainly, no end to the speech.

Fights and arguments at our house work according to the same principles. There is the point we are fighting about. It can be won or lost according to the rules of debate by marshaling arguments in favor or against the question, predicting the future, and alluding to experiences that might cast light on the issue. But since there is no judge present to bang down a gavel when our arguments go astray, and one argument is related to all other arguments in a marriage, the debate soon jumps over to other terrains, times, quarrels, and problems, some of them having long been resolved, or so we both thought. Everything becomes fair game, and the hotter the rhetoric, the greater the overall effect. There are moral high grounds and subversive insinuations, all of which are tempting to use.

In every argument, though, there are things that can't be said. Here is where you need to choose your words carefully and know when to keep quiet. And here is also where my problem begins. These little secrets are usually what is most known about the marriage, and they are in some ways its essential truth. It is as if all the stress points of the marriage meet at one point where one simple screw holds the entire house together. A few turns of the screw start the building wobbling on its foundation; a few too many turns brings the roof crashing down around the shoulders of husband and wife and any innocent bystanders. The greatest threat to marriage is the temptation to give the screw an extra turn just to see your partner squirm. It is as if I know that winning the battle will lose the war, but my lust is high for the immediate taste of victory, and so I bring myself down just to see my adversary crumble.

When I was a boy, I lived in Kaukauna, Wisconsin, on a hill overlooking the Fox River. There were train tracks on our side of the river, and we used to watch the enormous yellow and green diesels dragging their loads of pine logs and heavy machinery back and forth throughout the day. One summer we built a giant slingshot on the hill in the natural fork of two basswoods, strapping two bicycle tire inner tubes and a swatch of leather to the trees. It looked like a slingshot dropped by Jack's giant or a huge weapon from the Middle Ages used to breach castle walls. The slingshot was so powerful that we could launch rocks bigger than bricks halfway across the Fox. And, of course, we gave the freight cars of the passing trains considerable attention. They shrugged off the large stones stoically, so we were only temporarily amused.

We began to think about firing on the caboose or the engine, which, housing men, could be expected to generate more of a reaction. We knew we could safely fire at the boxcars, but we craved excitement, even though we knew that it would be too much for us to take. In the end we naturally gave in to temptation, and two very angry railroad men chased us for a mile without reward before returning to make short work of our monstrous toy. They kept on the lookout for us after that, and it was a long time before they forgot about us and we could again roam the hill freely.

Marriage is like this experience. There are certain things you can do or say with impunity, but they are not exciting enough, no matter how sensational they seem, and so you look for more dangerous targets. Finding them is as perilous as shooting at them because once you find them, you never fail to take aim and fire. The only thing that can save you after you fire is a lucky case of amnesia.

Husbands and wives wound each other with words. But somehow, if they are lucky, they find other words that cover over what they should not have said, and the hurt is bathed in warm water and bandaged in clean white linens. Sleep and forgetfulness overcome the wounded, and they collapse together into old habits and old names. They take to their bed and tumble into the blankets and sheets, sinking down through the mattress and the foundation, falling through the second story and then the first story, plunging into the basement and deeper still into the earth, where they burrow into a cozy and familiar place full of memories and dreams and common history. There husband and wife lodge through the long night of their discontent and arise together in the morning to attend to more important matters: the turning off of the alarm clock, the scratching of heads and scrubbing of faces, the choosing of wardrobe for children and themselves, the common table of their life.

Every husband and wife has special words to heal the wounds they inflict on each other. Some of these healing words are the same for everyone: "husband and wife," "father and mother," "you and me," "we." These were the words spoken to each other by a man and a woman whose happiness it was to circle by car one of the largest and bluest lakes on the face of the earth. They are the words by the grace of which I was born, began my marriage, and saw my children born. They will be the words, I pray, by which my children someday name their love.

In Praise of Doris Day

The two movies I remember most from my childhood are *The Guns of Navarone* and *That Touch of Mink*. My parents took me to both. This is not in itself unusual, since parents spend a fair amount of time taking their children to the movies, but these two films were ones my parents wanted to see, and that is why I remember them. *The Guns of Navarone* was memorable for its big guns. *That Touch of Mink* had Doris Day. I was only nine years old, but Doris Day was a wonder for a boy to behold. Her hinder side was packaged in haute couture, and Cary Grant chased after it. Bob Hope had said years before that you could play a nice hand of bridge on it. Her raspy voice was sexy and smart when she talked, ardent and truthful in song. When she was angry or being fussy, her foot in medium heel tapped the ground insolently. It was always for a just cause, and you knew it when you saw the look in her eyes. She was mother and lover rolled into one—a dangerous combination—sexy to her comfort level, a blonde in the age of platinum blondes who could be a blonde and keep her self-respect.

You only come to know a woman the second time you see her because the first time is only the wonderful reference point and it takes two points to get a line on someone. The second time I saw Doris Day was at the Cook family's house on television. I was baby-sitting for the Cooks' two children, and they were in bed sleeping. It was late at night, and I was downstairs in the living room in the dark, trying to watch *Love Me or Leave Me*. Doris Day played Ruth Etting to James Cagney's Marty Snyder; it was the story of a chorus girl on her way to the big time and the small-time hood who gave her a start. Watching her was not as easy as it might have seemed because I was all alone in the house, it was dark, and Mr. Cook had been a very successful hunter of birds in his younger years. The living room was mounted with a dozen stuffed birds of prey: hawks, eagles, and owls, but mostly owls—snow owls, barn owls, great horned owls. Some were in flight, balanced on the walls, claws extended, and others were perched above me, ready to leap at their prey. All of them seemed as interested in me as I was in the blonde singer on television.

I knew who Jimmy Cagney was. He was the guy who punched and danced and hit dames with grapefruit. Here he was a pathetic cripple and a gangster, his only virtue being that he loved Doris Day. That she could not love him was understandable, although she was a good enough person that she could not really understand it herself. She wanted to see in him the good that he saw in her, but he wanted her too much.

Jimmy Cagney was the guy who wanted the girl. He was willing to do everything to have her, but everything was too much. One good thing would have done the trick.

Doris Day was the girl who broke into song, and when she did, you knew why Cagney wanted her, and why he would never have her. She was too good.

I could not say at the time why I became a fan, but I kept an eye out for her movies without having made a resolution about it. I now see it as an expression of my desire to grow up and become a man, since Doris Day was a woman who could love only a man. In *Teacher's Pet* she played the teacher, and it was her ideal role because she always had something to teach you. She was the daughter of a famous newspaperman, whom she loved and remembered by teaching his understanding of newspapers. Clark Gable was a city editor who was taking her class under false pretenses to humiliate her. She turned out to be wrong about her father, from whom she had learned everything, but right in what she felt about him. Clark Gable failed to humiliate her and fell in love with her instead, and he was right, too. What I remember most about the film is how much he was in awe of her love of her father and how much he was in awe of her, so that he almost became a boy before her womanhood, until he woke up in the nick of time and remembered that he, too, was a newspaperman, that he knew a thing or two about the world, and that he, too, had something to offer her.

In *The Man Who Knew Too Much,* she was paired with James Stewart. She played, unexpectedly and uncharacteristically, a woman driven to hysteria by the kidnapping of her son. The level of hysteria projected by her, however, can't be explained solely by the plot, which is not unusual in itself for Alfred Hitchcock's films, because there is something else going on in her performance. What I usually liked about Doris Day was that the men around her always thought at first that she was a hysteric, or just another silly woman, but she never turned out to be one because she was right in the way she felt, and a hysteric is never right in the way she feels. Eventually, the men realized this about her, as if passing time with her was the equivalent of taking lessons in how to become a good judge of women and a good man.

But everything was different in this film. Jimmy Stewart was her husband and a doctor, and he was supposed to know her. So when he drugs her before telling her that their son has been kidnapped, and she fulfills his expectations by going crazy, it is a dark moment not only for the character but for Doris Day. Her craziness doesn't have any anger or rightful indignation in it; it is a madness of the body, empty of intelligence and grace. She loses control of her movements, expressions, and dignity, and Jimmy Stewart wrestles her clumsy body into bed. That he is a doctor makes it worse because it seems she married him only because she is a woman in constant need of one.

Hitchcock always seemed to be telling a story in which a woman risks to lose her soul to a man. Now he was trying to plunder Doris Day. He had taught Jimmy Stewart how to do it to Grace Kelly. In *Vertigo*, a few years later, he would change Kim Novak from a woman of grace into a thick-legged mannequin. I sometimes think Doris Day's atypical hysteria in this role may be explained merely by the fact that she is blonde and costarring in an Alfred Hitchcock movie with James Stewart. She knew what they wanted to do to her.

In the end, though, they don't get away with it, and she saves herself. They don't fail because her character is indomitable. In fact, the conclusion of the film only restores the status quo: she recovers her son, embraces him, and slips back into the role of slightly hysterical mother and wife, one who needs a husband with a bottle of pills handy. They fail to steal her soul only because she possesses something they can't take away from her: the ability to sing. It is not something you can pretend to have. It is not a matter of acting—what men often make women do for perverse enjoyment. Doris Day knows how to sing, and when she sings, it is the most singular moment in the movie. It is singular because it reveals that this beautiful woman, who is supposed to be talented and famous according to the script, but who never shows enough self-possession to make it believable, has magical powers of her own, beyond anyone else's control or imagining. I don't care much for "Que Sera, Sera." But when Doris Day sings it in the embassy scene, she transforms it into a heart-wrenching ballad. It is no longer a nursery rhyme for children, or for men who would remain children before women. She transfigures the song and it transfigures her. The voice rises out of her like the Holy Spirit, penetrating people and walls and rendering them harmless. The song is like a powerful but gentle light, a tongue of fire, emanating from an inner place of strength and resourcefulness—what can only be called her soul. The effect has nothing to do with the lyrics or melody of the song. The song is about untwistable fate, but Doris Day unmakes it with her voice and subjects fate to her will, changing what will be into what she requires.

For me, the scene is the pinnacle of Doris Day's career, although she has played better scenes and sung better songs, because it always brings me back to the moment when I first recognized her, as another singer of ballads, Ruth Etting in *Love Me or Leave Me*. She is the same graceful creature, surrounded by the same brutality and corruption, playing against the odds. In the end she crushes everything that is evil and sordid with her sincerity.

I have not thought about Doris Day for a long time. I suppose it is not very easy anymore to understand what she was—any more than it is easy to find a room full of stuffed owls. She retired from films at forty-four, after over twenty years on the screen, and devoted her life to her dogs. I imagine she lives among them still. She quit making films at a time when times were changing, and now those times are gone. Today women are not the same on film. Gone are Jean Arthur, Ginger Rogers, Irene Dunn, June

Allyson, and Doris Day. Actresses still play wives, girlfriends, and enterprising single women, but they are just as likely, more likely in fact, to play hookers, where they are required to display much more than hearts of gold, as if their entrée into film depended on getting a pinup taped into the fantasy scrapbook of some man who never grew up. Women on screen today are often pinups disdainful of men who like to look at pinups. But Doris Day was never a pinup, and it is hard to imagine her playing a call girl. In fact, she never played or appealed to men who could not grow up, and the actors with whom she starred were usually, with few exceptions, complete packages: James Cagney, Clark Gable, James Stewart, Cary Grant, James Garner, Rod Taylor, Brian Keith. Even at their weakest moments they were men, and they all knew and appreciated a good thing when they saw it.

Doris Day was always referred to as the girl next door. It was an epithet of respect. But when the sexual revolution came, they called her the girl next door and laughed at her, as if there were no longer girls in the neighborhood worth falling in love with and even the idea of it was silly. How anyone could see her and hear her and still laugh at her, I don't know. She was honest and trusting and natural. She was virtue itself and virtue's reward. She was a hard act to follow because she wasn't acting.

Women Are Like the Earth

If you lower your head below the horizon of your lover's body and study her contours, you will rediscover the lay of the land. Women are like the earth. There are postcards for sale in every seaside resort that make the local scenery look like the body of a woman. Sand blown into dunes, shaped round and lovely, is a woman's body. The sea rolling into the sea, cupped within itself, blue beneath and spread with foam, is a woman's body. A stand of leafless ash trees against a hill is a woman's body. I can find no photographs of natural formations that resemble a man's body. I don't dream this way. Perhaps I can't.

When a boy is born, he is laid on the belly of his mother. He sinks into her skin into the empty place of his birth. His knowledge of landscape begins there with his mother's body, the first country he knows inside and out. It is his America, his newfound land. He is fed by it before he knows that it is she. He is in love with it, and then he falls in love with her because she was it. He will spend his remaining days studying others in her image, falling in and out of love, scratching at the surface, trying to make an impression, lost on the outside. Always students of appearance are men. Never anything deeper. Never anything real.

Maybe this is why men love fellatio. They are dreaming they are real, for a change. They are mother earth, and they imagine women want to consume them, like a long loaf of bread, and their taste is good. Men dream about women as hungry as they are. Every sexual fantasy contains this hungry woman. Every sexual stereotype is a dream of her. Who are these women? They are goddesses who want to consume men as if they were fruit of the earth.

Magic Tricks

Two magic tricks always affect me. One is where the magician levitates a beautiful woman in midair and rings her body with a hoop to prove no strings are attached. The other is where the magician saws a woman in half and then puts her back together. The first trick is a fantasy where a man purges a woman of her sexual history and imagines a future when she belongs only to him. The second trick is a fantasy about a man satisfying a woman completely.

Men invented magic tricks because they think they need them to please women—and to please themselves, since men are most happy when they work some kind of sexual wonder on women. "If only I can find that magic button again," a man thinks as he rummages below his lover's belt. He is remembering that fortuitous event in the recent past when he really hit upon something special. But that little toggle switch doesn't work without the magic word. "Abracadabra!" No swoons. "Open sesame!" Still locked up tight. "I love you, baby!" She won't let him in. This magic doesn't seem to be working.

There are no magic tricks in making love. Love becomes magical only when you have given up the magician's art, when you no longer want to float her in the air or stretch her out on a table and saw her in half or pull long ribbons and many-knotted bows from her openings. Only when you no longer want to be a magic man will a silver coin drop from her mouth into your hand.

In the Cave of the Lovers

A man wants nothing more than to drag the woman he loves down into a cave. It is a cave as big as their two bodies, a hole hugging two bodies fused together. It is the cave of sex. It is the cave of the lovers.

The cave is a dark and scary place. It is a dark and lovely place. It is childhood revisited and entombed in ecstasy. It is a cradle of rhyme, rhythmic slaps, and poetry of the body.

> Hey, diddle, diddle!
> The cat and the fiddle,
> The cow jumped over the moon;
> The little dog laughed
> To see such sport,
> And the dish ran away with the spoon.

In the cave of the lovers, the two want always to be two while doing everything they can to be three. They make love all the time. Before and after meals, in the dark of night, in the dark of morning, in the sunny afternoon. They make love all the time.

The lovers are on a honeymoon where the moon swells and swells and refuses to wane. It is full and sticky. Its seas run with honey, marias black and golden with the effluvia of love.

The moon pushes into the cave. The moon is the cave. There will always be a glow of moonlight in the cave, always the scent of honey turning to sugar, always two bodies glued together.

And then there are three. Three is when it stops. Three is awakening and whispering after lust. Three is teardrops and tedium and humanity. Three is the unequal division of desire between love and sex. Three is life outside the cave. The cave is what every man imagines love with a woman will be, and then there are three.

Adam and Eve

Adam and Eve were in the habit of making love all the time. But they stopped. Adam felt like dreaming about Eve for a change. So he went to sleep and imagined she had changed into something ripe and beautiful, her flesh white and juicy, her skin red and tight. Meanwhile, Eve started to get hungry. She left Adam's side and went for a stroll around the garden to look for a bite to eat—for something beautiful and bright to nourish her. But you don't need to eat in paradise any more than you need to dream. In paradise all you need is paradise. In paradise all you need is man and woman.

But Adam and Eve got tired of being man and woman all the time. They got hungry for something else. This something else appeared in the form of an apple. Perfectly round and red, as magical as a dream, it materialized on the branch of a tree. Eve took the first bite and then Adam took a bite. That's when the angel with the flaming sword drove them from paradise.

Lust (Always an Incomplete Story)

I enter a room, angular and sprawling, lit only by low table lamps. Long funnels of light open upon the ceiling. Shadows run down the walls to narrow peaks, dark triangles of gray blue fringed in yellow. A chance to see a tassel. Among still bodies, bodies, bodies on low black stools move, iridescent in flashes and turns, like long fish held and released by strong currents on the bottom of a stream, slippery black rocks under their bellies, fins darting among the ooze.

I ask her to show me her private things, the things she is embarrassed to have. Then I lie down on the floor, flat on my back, and wait.

Moving behind, behind, behind, never catching up to her cries.

The Men a Woman Knows

The number of men a woman knows is easy to count. Count how many sons she has and you will know how many men she knows. The only men who allow themselves to be known by a woman are her sons. Men, to be fair about it, don't know any women. They certainly don't know their daughters, although the daughters don't seem to mind it because they are in love.

In the Metro of the Mind

The subways of the world, whether in New York, London, or Paris, cut paths that lead not so much underground as to the unconscious mind. The New York subway is a cave of fear where I feel like a victim. I watch everyone while pretending to see nothing. The London tube teaches patience and duty. I think of myself as on the job and stay on the lookout for my stop. The Paris metro is a tunnel of love. It is a world of sexual thrills and dangers where the men fantasize about the women, and the women, I imagine, do the same thing. I never know what the women in my car expect of me, if they expect anything at all. I try not to think about them. I usually end up not thinking about them a lot until I exit into the light of day.

Not long ago, I found myself sitting across from a young woman in the metro. She had a very unusual handcrafted briefcase on her lap. It had under a first flap three pockets in which she was neatly arranging her things. I had never seen anything like it. I thought I would like to have one myself, and I looked at it with interest. When I glanced up at her, I saw that she was looking at me. She became uncomfortable, as if I had violated her. I took out a book and began to read, taking care not to look in her direction again.

When the train arrived at my stop, I saw that she stood up before me to get out, and I found myself behind her at the door. I didn't want her to think that I was following her. I thought she would probably cut left to the main exit once she got off the train, while I planned to take the less frequented exit to the right. To my dismay, she turned toward my exit, and I knew I would be walking up the stairs behind her. Out of nowhere a band of five rowdy young men intercepted us and stood between us on the stairway. They commented on her aloud. I planned strategies to help her if they should become more violent. I tried to assess the strength of each man and his willingness to fight. I imagined myself in a battle with them. I'd pull a few of them backwards down the stairwell to reduce their numbers. I'd fight off the rest with my fists. And, of course, she would be grateful. Suddenly she turned to the left, where I turn to the right. The men turned left behind her. I walked to the far stairwell, climbed the stairs deliberately, and emerged into the light of day.

Part 4: Man to Man, Mostly to Himself

Teasing

A long time ago, when I was yet a college student, I visited a girlfriend at her parents' home in Milwaukee. She was the girl with whom I had had to that date the most intense physical relationship—and the most disastrous. I was very much in love with her, but I was unable to control myself long enough to show her how much, and she eventually left me for a kinder man. It was a January afternoon, close to the holidays and uncommonly warm. We went for a walk in the sparse woods near her house, as lovers are pledged to do, whether they are staying with parents or not. I remember the stark contrast of the woods: young ash trees, black and chunky with bark, grew amid the patches of wet white snow; the crunch of our footsteps on the frozen leaves punctuated the silence. We were talking as we walked, heads inclined together, hand in hand, when I brushed against a thorn bush. The thorns were long and pronounced and already the color of blood just before it hardens to a scab. I snapped one of them off the branch and menaced her with it in a teasing way. I was not really serious about sticking her at first. Then she moved abruptly away from me, as if she didn't trust me, and I pursued her with it. My idea—and she knew it—was to stab her in the softness of her hinder. I lunged to deliver the thorn, but she put her hands behind her to block it, and the thorn entered into the smallest finger of her right hand at the root between the two fingers. She screamed, I stopped, and when she removed her woolen gloves, I saw the thorn had broken off to leave a bluish splinter deep beneath the surface of the skin. Later I dug long and painfully with a sewing needle to retrieve it. It was in a painful spot and it was in much too deep. We had to stop before it was out because she could no longer stand holding her hand open to the needle.

On another occasion, many years later, I was visiting a cottage on a small lake in northern Michigan. My wife and son had gone out in the boat to do some fishing and to tour the chain of lakes. I was abandoned on shore with my five-year-old daughter, and we went wading together for the very first time. She was timid about the water, so I took her up on my back. She clung to me like a little monkey in a combination of affection and fear, and I felt a physical closeness and oneness with her I have not often felt. It was early evening. The sun was beginning to go down into the lake. It reflected at low angles off the surface of the water, blinding me and warming my face. I waded out toward the yellow boat markers, and we peered together toward the horizon, shielding our eyes and searching the line of water and sky like a pair of ancient mariners. As we advanced, I tipped my body from side to side to let her feet trail in the water, and little by little I got the idea that she should try to do some wading herself. It would help her to get over her fear of deep water; I could teach her a few swimming strokes. Or so beat the refrain. So I asked her whether she wanted to climb down, but she was either too afraid or enjoying herself too much on my back.

Then I began to play at letting her fall off my back into the water. I stooped low so that a wave might splash her. I pretended to lose my grip on her. At first, my teasing intensified the pleasure of having her on my back because she scrambled to hold on tighter, breathing on my neck and gripping me in her tiny arms. Very soon I was teasing her for real, churning up the water with high steps, pretending to stumble over imaginary rocks, letting my grip on her slacken until she felt she would fall. I didn't throw her into the water but I did spoil one of the more memorable moments of my life because I could not overcome my desire to tease.

Whatever these two memories mean—and I could, unfortunately, provide worse—they seem to tell in part about my own evil and the evil of men. Teasing is for me a sinister hunger. I crave it as I crave meat, water, or sex, and so I imagine it as the eighth deadly sin. Perhaps you will think I am exaggerating. I wish it were true. Not many people believe in evil these days. We have as a species spent a great deal of our thoughts and words about it, and now our pockets are empty. And yet there is something either out there or here in my breast that craves disorder and ruin.

In better theological days, we used to call this impulse a "temptation." I think most people, among them the best theologians, have not understood temptation very well because they think it is an inclination to turn away from the good. When I am being tempted, however, I am not looking for something evil. I am peering out at a horizon of distant and merging reflections, as I was that evening with my daughter, looking for something good and beautiful; but somehow the goodness turns into ugliness when I reach for it.

This is what happens in teasing. The tease starts out with an idea of goodness. He is happy, even jubilant, but he ruins his happiness for the promise of another happiness. This other happiness is a false joy, blocking the rightful path to what is good and true and beautiful. He enters a dark tunnel with eyes focused ahead—not in the present where the body must remain and the hand steals the forbidden thing from another's heart or hand. If we could understand the impulse to tease, we might see that human evil is a blind attraction, a hunger, and that all thoughts of evil deliver us into chaos and sadness with the promise of happiness.

You will ask how we may know true happiness from false happiness, or when to set our lights by our ambitions or risk a little happiness for more happiness. I don't know. I think, somehow, that the sleeper who dreams beautiful dreams only to return to a degrading reality is less fortunate than one who drowns in nightmares and struggles toward wakefulness out of breath and terrified to be comforted by life. To have visions of unhappiness, evil, and cruelty that reveal your life to be far better than you might have wished is as good an idea of paradise as anyone might possess. Perhaps this is why Dante pictures Satan as a huge icy giant, motionless and apparently asleep, except for the instinctive grinding of his jaws, into which Brutus, Cassius, and Judas Iscariot have been thrown by God. Satan lies frozen in sleep at the black core of the Inferno satisfied in his dreams of ruling paradise, only to be awakened from hellish moment to hellish moment by the bitter taste of traitors befouling his mouth. Far above him hosts of heavenly angels, each identical to every other, toss and turn all night long in beds of gold, dreaming that they are mere mortals, each depraved and lost to a different sin. They open their eyes every morning in unison to see before them the spectacle of their thousand perfect twins looking back with relief.

The main reason for the ugliness of teasing is that it almost always occurs among friends or family. Few people will dare to tease a stranger. Teasing requires intimacy, and the greater the desire for intimacy, the greater is the temptation to tease. This means that the victims of teasing are hurt by the people they most love and trust and, worse, that these people, who do love their victims, don't in the end seem to care enough about them to keep faith with their love. It is this situation that permits teasing to persist over a period of months and years, and that it can go on for so long without anyone noticing or objecting to it, except for the victim, shows how insidious and destructive it can be. Teasing breaks down a person like nothing else, and it can demoralize you for a lifetime.

What unites the tease and his victim is ultimately nothing like love or intimacy but only the determination of the tease, who will not let up no matter what. Once the tease finds a chink in the other person's armor, he begins to tear into it, and he makes sure that his victim knows he is going for blood. The victim is subject to the tease's will and exists only to have his or her will undone. What the tease craves is this undoing: a taste of victory and knowledge. The victory is the victory over the prey. The knowledge the tease craves is his victim's realization that he or she has been undone. It is a game of hide and seek where the victim doesn't want to play, runs away all the harder because of it, and becomes a better fox to chase. This makes teasing different from playing or organized games where the object of the hunt is in agreement with the game, and there are rules to protect everyone. In teasing, there is only one rule: the teasing stops only when the victim loses the powers of resistance, when he or she is broken or opened, when the victim is in effect dead.

It is rare for teasing to go this far, of course, and yet all teasing reaches in spirit for death. Fortunately, there is usually someone, perhaps a special emissary of God, who intervenes and stops the tease. It is as if the angels cry out at the sight of you, and you see the image of your crime reflected in the mirror of an angel's eye:

a man in a lake dangles a small girl over the blue water; a young woman runs from a thorn and her lover amid thin black trees and melting snow.

I am more of a tease than a victim, and it has always been so. As a child, I teased my younger brother without mercy. I dominated him as I have never dominated anyone before or since, and as I would hope never to dominate anyone ever again. I can't give examples, although I am sure he can, because shame has erased my cruelest memories. All I remember is the empty feeling of having been a torturer, and even this memory is too sickening for me to think about for any amount of time. The best I can do is to picture the obscene forms, seen in the eye of an angel, of two boys transformed by the evil of teasing, one voluntarily, the other against his will. One is the color of a thorn; he looms with grasping hands and eyes over the other, who—yellow and blue—has been opened.

Shopping for Time

I am not much of a shopper. I shop but I don't shop for the pleasure of it. I tend to decide what I want and go get it. It is true that I venture on occasion into the local shopping mall with Jill to meander through the crowds, window-shopping, lollygagging, ambling from store to store to no purpose, and then stopping for a cup of coffee in a bad fast-food restaurant. It is a civic duty to go to the town square from time to time, if only to catch a glimpse of your fellow citizens. Such occasions, though, are for me the exception rather than the rule.

The one time I do remember shopping for shopping's sake was in college. I was an undergraduate at the University of Wisconsin in Madison, and it happened that the university hospital had the best cancer ward in the state. My mother was dying of lymphoma—or so we thought at the time—she lived to die of ovarian cancer a decade later. They had recently removed a tumor from the side of her head the size and color of an orange, and with it most of the matter of her left eye. I think it was her left eye. I have trouble remembering which one it was because I can't seem to get behind her eyes long enough to fathom her right side from her left. I have to map her wounds by imagining her looking at me and then turn my right side into her left side and so forth. But when I imagine her looking at me, I would rather try to talk with her than make the calculation. So I can never say whether she lost her right or left eye.

I thought she was going to die even though the immediate danger was over. I was spending a lot of time with her at the hospital because I loved her and because the rest of my family lived up north and could only make their way down on weekends. I felt that I had to be with her all the time. But on this day, I was told by the doctor to delay my arrival at the hospital. I didn't know what to do with myself. I felt numb and generally unfit. There was too much time before I had to go to the hospital, and yet I felt like time was running out. To pass the time or to save it, I am not sure which, I went shopping on State Street. I passed through many shops, looking in earnest to buy something. I remember specifically trying not to buy just anything but to concentrate my thoughts on buying something special.

I eventually found myself in a men's store, a very traditional and, to my wallet, expensive one. I bought a navy blue crew neck Shetland wool sweater. It was at the time the most expensive sweater I had ever bought, and penny for pound, given inflation and time, it may be the most expensive sweater I own. And I own many sweaters.

I wore the sweater when I went to visit her. I felt it was somehow for her as much as for myself. I still have it, and it is my only sweater whose elbows I have patched when they became worn rather than throwing it away. I asked Jill to pick out and sew on the blue suede patches as a kind of memorial gesture to my mother and as a tribute to herself. The only other time I ever had a sweater with patched elbows was as a boy, when my mother saved my then-favorite sweater from oblivion by coming up with and executing the idea of patching the elbows with leather. I wanted my blue sweater to recall this occasion and Jill to take the place of my mother in the memory. Even now when a patch on my blue Shetland comes loose and needs to be sewn, I ask Jill to take care of it, even though I could do it myself, because I want it to remain her concern alone.

My first favorite sweater was very warm and very green, and I eventually grew out of it. And so I lost it to oblivion after all. I will never grow out of my blue Shetland sweater, and I hope to keep it in good repair for a long time.

The Mandolins of St. Jean de Luz

I have lived in St. Jean de Luz, a small Basque coastal village in the southwest of France, for only one month, but I dream of finishing my days there. Actually I have lived in St. Jean two times for a month—always the same month, the month of June, because June is less expensive and crowded than July and because August, being the national vacation month in France, is the most expensive and crowded of all. I don't know St. Jean well, but each time I have lived there the same things have happened. That is why I dream of finishing my days there. I want to give up on making things different. I want to give up on the ambition of beginning and the egotism of ending. In St. Jean only the beginning and end matter because everything in between is the same.

My days are spent in the same places, beginning and ending the same trips and tasks. I move between the city and the sea, morning, noon, and night. The morning is for going to the market and wondering at the ferocious waters and startling rocks at the point of farthest incursion of land into sea. The afternoon is for visiting the graveyard on the hill overlooking the town or lying on the beach, so abundant with children, their sand pails, and sleeping mothers. The evening is for shifting among festivalgoers and listening to the waves on the pitch-dark shore. At midnight the children fall asleep in their rooms, and I sit with Jill at a game of cards until the cards drop to the table and our hands seek out each other.

I have seen this morning before. I rise to buy a loaf of bread, maybe some coffee and jam. It never rains in the morning, so the street is dry. The baker knows what I will order and I know how much to pay her. The bread is still warm when I return home and we eat it with jam and black coffee mixed with hot milk. If it is market day, after breakfast I go to the market. I buy olives and cherries. I buy *brebis*, a cheese milder and less brittle than parmesan, made from the milk of sheep. I buy *rillettes de canard* and a bottle of Irouleguy—a dark local wine with a cassis perfume. The fish is always good, the tomatoes sweeter than any other place on earth, the people somehow wiser. A vendor sees that my daughter is unhappy. Mosquitoes are eating her alive every night, and her face is swollen with bites. He breaks off a stalk of leeks, crushes the stems, and tells us to apply the juice to her bites. We do it and she feels better immediately. The children see ducklings in three sizes, pet them all, and gawk at a skinned calf's head, its eyeballs staring blankly like an old man's.

If it is not market day, we walk to the farthest point of land and stand on the cliff above the sea. The waves are large and wild, and we can see even greater waves crashing in the distance. When we reach the point, we circle around the hill to the shore so we can catch a glimpse of the ocean beyond the sea wall. We notice right away that the ocean is enraged by ships but not by human beings. Two large military ships have sought safe harbor in the bay, yet the surfers are out there seeking thrills. Young boys of thirteen and fifteen, dressed in wet suits, work their way over the rocks and then thrust their boards out toward the immense ships. We climb down the rocks to the sea wall to contemplate the giant cliff. We are splashed several times but not carried away. We see the enormous cliff, eroded in geometrical patterns, while the huge waves break against it, continuing the work of the ages. The sea wall turns the surf against itself, driving the waves at right angles against the incoming ones, shooting huge watery blue twists into the air. The children climb into the crevices to have their picture taken, and my son pounds a stone against the cliff wall, breaking off pieces of shale in sympathy with the sea.

Three o'clock arrives again, and if the weather is warm, I find myself lying on the beach. Nothing ever happens on the beach. The beach is a mental landscape where bodies move and recline on the stage of thought. Two women lounge on the rocks to my immediate right, raking their long hair with their fingers and rubbing each other with oil, which makes their skin glisten like the scales of a silver fish. A bachelor, impeccably pumped up, inspects them while pretending to inspect himself. In the distance, a slender girl takes up a position on the rise above us. Her face beams with inexperience and expectation. Suddenly a helicopter, chopping at the air and beating up the surf, appears in the blue sky over the water. Airmen drop lines down to a military ship below and haul up sailors who later jump out of the helicopter into the bay. This is repeated many times. No one on the beach watches it. They are more interested in watching their neighbors roll over in the sand or adjust their swimsuits.

I have been lying in the heat for an eternity. The children run off and come back to me, mimicking the ocean waves. They pester me for cookies and apples and water to drink. Then the clouds come in. Although the light has dimmed, it is as if someone has turned on a light because the glare is cut and you can see the beach clearly for the first time. The faces of people, their swimsuit patterns, and distant beach umbrellas suddenly leap into focus. The two mermaids sunbathing near me are suddenly revealed to be mere human females with heavy hips and short legs. Gray hairs appear on the chest of the brilliantly bronzed bachelor. The lines of middle age now wrinkle the face of the young girl in the distance.

If the wind is cold over the beach, we spend an hour in the afternoon at the cemetery overlooking the village. Among the tidy family plots are found others, long abandoned, with broken crosses and flowerpots, heaps of bricks and masonry left by workmen, and various plastic bottles. I am beginning to know the names on the tombstones, and from what I can tell the earliest burial was 1890. One of the oldest tombs is an obelisk—very impressive from a distance, but when you get close, you see that the wrought iron fence is rusted, the door is a slab of sheetrock, and the inside is cluttered with broken coffins. The children like to go to the cemetery, but they like better to leave it. Soon they will look upon graveyards as a place to go at night to get away from their parents. Eventually they will know people buried in them, and the authority of the dead will be inescapable.

Every evening is like the last until the last evening comes. Jill dresses in Basque colors, the hues of night and blood, and I show a taste of them, too. We want to watch the closing ceremonies, including the Fires of St. John, but the weather is bad and we are uncertain about the hour. We hurry through the rain to the center of town, and when we arrive, we are happy to discover that the tree at the main square has not yet been set afire. Everywhere else in Christendom trees are used as symbols of birth. Not in St. Jean. The Basques mark the conclusion of the rites of St. John by burning their trees and their beginnings. Everyone turns out to watch. They chase after the flying sparks and try to collect them before they burn out because legend tells that an ember that dies in your hand brings good luck until the Fires of St. John burn bright the next year.

We press against the barrier and get a good view of the small tree. Soon a band makes its way down the street and the fire brigade moves into position to set the fire. A team of dancers rings the tree as it burns and we crowd closer with everyone else. The wind blows up at several points, sending burning ashes and cinders into the crowd. The firemen make a human fire wall to protect us, their black slickers alive with the brilliant light of the yellow and red flames. As soon as the fire has burned down, the fire brigade begins to douse the tree. But the crowd has other ideas: we run toward the black and glowing remains of the tree to gather up the hot embers. I find a small ember the size of a child's finger. When it has cooled, I put it in the center of the notebook in my coat pocket.

Then the musicians on the main stage of the band shell strike up, and fugitive bands prowl the square. Jill spots a table at the Madrid Café that is almost protected by the awning. We run over and the waiter wipes off the seats. Just as we sit down, a tremendous downpour begins. The waiter grabs our table and wedges it farther under the canopy while reassuring everyone that the storm will pass quickly. It does by the time we are ready to order. A second band strikes up, and the villagers come out to dance in front of the band shell. Then the rain pours down ferociously and everyone scatters. The rain stops and everyone reappears. We stay until we begin to fall asleep.

I lie in bed awaiting sleep. Sleep arrives. It is so dark and deep. Not a speck of light contradicts the darkness of it. Then I awaken to a distant melody, stopping and starting, moving closer little by little, steady now, now louder, steady again, growing louder. It sounds like a song on a car radio. The driver doesn't know where he is going. He is too old. He stops his car at every corner, each time forgetting his way home, falling deep into thought, and then remembering to drive on to the next corner. He keeps forgetting and remembering his way home at every stop sign, as if the sign means "Stop Remembering" and then "Stop Forgetting."

The music is coming from a troop of wandering mandolin players nestled beneath our window. They play sweetly, as music can only be played in the night. There is no more beautiful sound than the music of the mandolin, unless it be the music of two mandolins. The instrument seems capable of rendering classical phrasing almost as well as the violin, and yet it has at other moments the ability to mimic the coarse folksy strains of the guitar. The melody dies, and the musicians move a block up the street and begin to play again.

I return to bed, wanting to listen to them through the bedroom window as they wander away. A tremendous thunder erupts in the distance, a storm blows in, and a powerful rain sweeps overhead. The mandolins fall silent. I feel fully awake. I spoon with Jill, which makes me want to sleep even less, but I don't want to wake her. Then I hear the mandolins again in the distance. Perhaps I am hearing them only in my mind, hoping that the rain has not defeated them. The music is too faint to tell.

I am on the plane back to America. The engines of the plane have stirred time to nothing, but I am thinking about a moment somewhere in time—a time when my father is alive, a time when my father is not. I have been calling him from St. Jean but he doesn't answer. It is his birthday, very early in the morning for him, and he should be at home. I wait twenty minutes to call again. Still no answer. I wait another twenty minutes—no answer—and another fifteen. It is daybreak when he finally comes to the phone, but he thinks it is dusk and wishes he could have his supper. I wish him a happy birthday. He is surprised because he doesn't remember it is his birthday. I tell him I will be returning to America on June 26. He writes down the date. Then we talk about his birthday again and he guesses at the day. He reasons that he must have been born on June 26. I tell him the right date, June 7, and he writes it down, no doubt next to the other one.

For a moment, he comes to himself and tells me that my brother called to wish him a happy birthday. Then he is gone, and the man on the phone is no longer my father.

When I reach America, perhaps I will see him. I am in the middle of my life, and in the middle, moments crash together and are confused. Things are unclear this far from the beginning and the end, and the straight way is lost. I remember another moment that may have happened. I put the heat on because our rooms are chilly and the children are cold. Then I climb down the stairs to the streets of St. Jean. I sit in the little square next to St. Elisabeth's Church and watch the villagers go by. I try to match styles and ages. Many older people dress like youngsters or let themselves go completely. There must, I think, be a middle ground. The shop directly across from me has a mirrored front. I look like a stranger to myself. I have a nice tan, but it makes my hair look completely gray. I am reminded of a story by Isak Dinesen called "The Old Chevalier." Youth disappears, she says, when you realize that everything is not possible in your life and that miracles will not happen for you any more. Then you see you are the same as everyone else. I still want to believe that a star shines its light on me from above, but I am beginning to think it is only egotism. If losing your youth means you see yourself as being the same as everyone else, perhaps the fear of egotism is the first step toward old age.

As I lie in bed listening to the mandolins playing in the night, I think I might find no better thing to do with my remaining years than to learn to play the mandolin well. I will give up on miracles. I will give up on trying to make new beginnings and new endings. I will forget myself and remember the mandolin.

There is one thing I have not mentioned about St. Jean de Luz. It is the most important thing, as usual. The first time I was in St. Jean my father was dying. The second time, my father was dead, and I came to understand that I am dying.

Anger

If all men lived among the Eskimos—and if the landscapes of the polar north and polar south were as fiery as they can be frigid—then men would have a thousand and one words not for snow but for anger. As it is, angry men must content themselves with a handful: grief, anguish, and fear; fury, wrath, and rage; indignation, exasperation, and resentment; belligerence, irritation, and temper. We live in a world where the anger of men is seen as one vice only, where no one but the angry man understands its many emotional complexions. An angry man is only an angry man, as surely as a rose is only a rose, only a rose.

I have been an "angry boy" and an "angry young man." I am now an "angry man," and I will be, no doubt, an "angry old man"—at least until senility wraps me in its dreary and peaceful blanket. I have been angry as long as I can remember. But I have been angry about a thousand and one things, so all of my rages have felt different—here the tingling rawness of irritation, there the stony paralysis of regret, there again the gorgeous flowering of resentment. To call my rages, all, by the name of "anger" would make them the same and make me an "angry man." But I do not want to be an "angry man." I want only to be a man who tries not to get angry and who fails. But that is not the man I am. I am an "angry man."

And so I am angry as only a man can be, or a boy, since boys already possess the anger of men. Or perhaps men never get over the anger of boys. I had a terrible temper as a child, and an angry child lives within me still. I remember the rage surging through me, and I remember being told to control myself. In the third grade a kindly nun took me aside outside our classroom in the dark hall lined with the statues of saints to ask me whether I was turning into a bully. One of the mothers of my classmates had called St. Mary's to complain about me. It was a malicious act on her part because she lived across the street from us and the event she complained about happened on a Sunday evening and had nothing whatsoever to do with the life of the school. All the boys in the neighborhood had been playing in a yard of freshly mowed grass, sliding on the damp lawn and having grass fights. Besides throwing grass into my face, which was very much part of the game, one boy had grabbed repeatedly at my crotch. Even though he was bigger than I, I attacked him and we wrestled in the damp grass until I maneuvered him into a headlock, where I held him with such force and for so long that he nearly passed out. The next day he was unable to go to school, and that was when his mother called to complain about me.

In that dim hall among the saints I denied being a bully—as if any bully thinks of himself as one. In truth, I wasn't a bully, because my anger erupted in reaction to events and not to ignite them, and I usually felt justified in my violence and unashamed of it afterward. The nun's asking me if I was a bully so humiliated me, though, that I made a conscious and deliberate decision to master myself. I worked hard to gain control of my temper, and I felt for years that I had. My friends began to comment on my peaceful nature, and when we first met, Jill saw my even disposition as a stabilizing force in her life. My anger would still erupt from time to time, but it seemed under control, a safety mechanism especially designed to deal with extraordinary circumstances and not part of my real personality.

But something happened to me when my mother died and my father lost his reason and my children grew older. Now I want to throw things. At the moment when I have the greatest responsibilities, when I should be most mature and reasonable, I feel the most irresponsible and childlike. Something primitive has returned to take command of me with a power greater than ever before. It sweeps over me like the mistral, the hot wind that blows over the south of France. No life lives in it, and in its wake fly the mosquitoes, bloodless and thirsty for blood.

My life has been given over to anger, to avoiding it, to quenching and venting it. Sometimes, I am sad to say, my children are its victims. I am a man who loves to make plans, but there is no planning around children. They fall in the street on the way to a parade and begin to cry. They want to go home when they should want to stay and vice versa. It is not their fault. They are children. I have no such excuse when I throw a tantrum. Isn't it wrong to get angry at children? Don't you become a child yourself when you do?

Becoming a parent can be the final leaving behind of childhood, as parents die, depriving us of our old ideas, and children are born to replace us. Or, becoming a parent can be a repetition of childhood as we relive old lessons and fears. We carry our children within us as the children we once were as surely as we carry our children in our arms. But this means that our arms, the cradle of the body, are the place of adulthood. How do we reconcile old bodies and old arms with the interior life of the child? As the blood of the child rises in anger, the arms of the adult must remain steady and fast. As the voice of the child climbs, the voice of the adult must grow soft and wise.

This is the ideal picture. How rarely do I achieve it. I am afraid I will hurt my children and consider myself lucky I have not. Once when I was scrubbing the bathroom floor, my three-year-old daughter came to the doorway to watch me. She pushed the door open and it swung against me where I was kneeling, catching my toes under it. Without thinking, I kicked the door backward and it slammed on her fingers. I could feel in the vibration of the door the spongy resistance of her fingers in the doorjamb. I don't know what surprised her more, my sudden violence or the pain from her hand. She looked at me stupefied before bursting into tears.

My young son jumps from nowhere into my lap as I am reading and his knee kicks me in the groin. I throw him to the floor. His head narrowly misses the corner of the coffee table.

My daughter steps on the heel of my shoe as we are walking down the street. My shoe comes off, and I turn around and bark at her like a dog.

Anger is small and it is big. It makes the big man smaller and the small man bigger. This power to transform makes anger dangerous. It's why we call it a vice and are tempted to call it a virtue. On the one hand, the man who suffers from anger withdraws into a dark pit that is himself. There he ignites small fires that burn hotter than the space permits; they are not lit for comfort or for light but in anticipation of setting bigger fires to serve as weapons and to soothe his wounded pride. In the end, though, he uses his own pride for fuel, and he is consumed by the flames meant for his enemies. On the other hand, small boys grow angry out of frustration or lack of common sense without having any pride to wound. They fight to test each other and themselves, and their anger can help them to develop pride in themselves as men. This is why anger is valued in boys and young men as often as it is condemned. Anger either makes the man or destroys him. It is the volatile but indispensable ingredient poured on boys to make men.

My grandfather was a mason and a carpenter. He was often mean and always angry. He was angry when he was sober and angrier still when he was drunk. But he was also a man who, drunk or sober, exacted goodness from himself and those around him, and anger was part of the goodness. He put in foundations, block by block, wedged in hand-dug trenches on gravel bases and stacked up to the brim of the topsoil, and when the building inspector arrived, he never bothered to check whether the foundation was in square. He knew everything was true, and had to be, because my grandfather had laid the block with his own hands.

This was the same man who spat tobacco out the front window of his Ford and saw it whip around to splash across the faces of his sons in the back seat and who refused to close the rear window and laughed about it. This was the same man who told his wife to hang herself if she didn't like his drinking, and who was only a little sorry later when her sons pulled her down from the rafters in the garage where she tried to do it with her own belt.

When he lost his mind, my grandmother parked him in the corner chair in the parlor like a huge knickknack. His unruly temper was stilled by madness, and there he sat, gripping the arms of the chair with his powerful hands, all scrubbed, powdered, and diapered like a huge baby, eyes vacant, mouth ajar, finally in good humor. My grandmother used to point at him and complain that she finally had him where she wanted him. "He stays put now and behaves himself. But look at him."

My own father was filled with anger, but he was always kind to his children. Having been beaten by a man whose father beat him, he turned his anger against itself and refused to hurt his own sons and daughters. He was a small man, however, and he used his anger to double his size. Sometimes it also doubled his brain power. One night I was wrestling in the living room with my brother, Rob. The television set was jiggling and the lamps were swaying. My father told us to stop. But, of course, we didn't listen to him. My mother said, "Boys, your father told you to stop fighting." We didn't hear a word. Dad got up calmly and went out the back door and into the garage. A few minutes later he came back into the living room with an ax. Now he had our attention. He threw the ax into the middle of the living room and boomed, "Why don't you use an ax? Why don't you just break up the goddamn furniture with an ax?"

As children we feared our father until we were old enough to see what his anger had accomplished for him and how he used it. It made him successful as a small man, and to succeed as a small man is no small thing in a world of big men. I see now that my father was somehow happy in his anger, that it was a sign of his determination and self-worth, that he needed it. He let no one humiliate him, although he was not above humiliating himself. Perhaps this is one definition of a man—someone who takes responsibility for his own humiliation.

Eventually my father came to the same place as his father. He sat in a chair, staring blankly into space, eyes turned inward into himself. His rage had driven him further than anyone could have imagined. He kept swinging as long as he could until his mind was filled with nothing but anger. Then the anger ate his brain and he stopped throwing punches. He withdrew into himself completely, into a bountiful world full of cool places and gentle emotions, where hell on earth became, I hope, a pleasure.

One of my prized possessions is a Yankee hand drill. It is lightweight, will drill anything but metal, including plaster, and works extremely well for small jobs. The drill bits are self-storing in the handle and varied enough to cut holes small and large. My father filched it from his father. I don't remember the exact story, but somehow the theft had to do with a fight between them. My grandfather had come at my father for something, but by then the boy had become a man, and he told my grandfather he'd better not try to lay a hand on him. My grandfather laid a hand, and Dad knocked him to the ground. Grandfather got up and walked away, but he didn't talk to Dad for a long time. So Dad took the Yankee drill.

I have the drill now, but I didn't have to throw a punch for it. My father gave it to me, perhaps because he felt bad about the way he got it and didn't want to put me in the position of ever having to take something from him that way. It wasn't necessary because I'd never been tempted to strike my father, but perhaps he knew more about anger than I do. Anger makes you do things without ever tempting you to do them first.

I intend to pass the Yankee drill down to my own son, if I don't lose it or break it first. He will need it. He is quick tempered, and his anger is strong and lasting. It is the anger of my father and of his father. It is my anger. He will become a man or stay a boy because of it. When I see my young son furious with anger, I don't know what to think or feel. I feel guilty, and I feel proud.

Grown Men Don't Cry

It is a long time since I have cried. Most men can say this at any given moment and be telling the truth. A long time passes between tears when you are a man because grown men don't cry.

The last time I cried was in 1989. I was driving along an old river road that was once the main thoroughfare between two small towns in northeastern Wisconsin. The old road curves and turns with the river, seeking out the flatness of the ancient riverbed and mimicking the motion of tides long lost. Now the road connects the homes of people living along the river to the two towns. These people are the only ones, except for young lovers, who use it. I was on the road alone because it is also the shortest route between the town and the home beside the river where my father was then institutionalized. The road is solitary and beautiful, a place without distractions of traffic or commerce, where one can drive with too many thoughts or without a single thought and still hold to the center line. And yet one night after leaving my father in his dull and brainless world, buzzing with idiotic chatter and the drone of fluorescent lights, it turned out for me to be a road I could not navigate, and I had to pull off into the grass. I sat there for a long time before I could make my way home again to the empty house that once belonged to my father. But no more. Nothing belonged to him any more.

Tears don't go together with men. Everyone knows it, and men know it best of all. Efforts are made to praise the tears shed by men, as if somehow men might be improved or saved by learning how to cry. Men will never be saved by tears, though, only lost, for a man cries only when he is lost.

Listen to the sobs of a man. There is no music to his crying, nothing pure or beautiful. Women sometimes weep, their voices harmonizing with their tears, dissolving into the musical changes of flowing water. And if they are lucky, their cries wash away the pain. But male sobs don't wash away the pain because they are more painful than the wounds that cause them. Men cry against crying. Their sobbing is distorted by the struggle not to cry out, by grunts and groans uttered only under the exertions of heavy labor.

Observe the body of a crying man. It is at war with itself. Men don't tear open their own bodies, as grieving women do, trying to make an exit for their anguish. Their bodies don't give out or relax when they cry; they don't spread themselves on the bed or fall at length to the floor. They jackknife in two, compressing themselves into a ball, knotting their arms back over their heads to stop their brains from exploding out of the back of their skull. They clench their teeth and twist their arms to straitjacket themselves. This struggle is apparent even in little boys, whose tiny bodies shake when they cry and whose tears are already salted with self-contempt.

It is not that men don't want to cry in public. Men don't refuse to cry because someone is watching. They cry the same whether in private or in public. The agony is part of them, not caused by the circumstances. Boys cry and are told it is not manly, so they stop crying out of the desire to become men. But by the time they have become men, they have stopped crying for another reason—it is too painful and humiliating not to be in control of yourself.

There are those who think that men should be able to have a good cry. They think men should let it all hang out when it comes to crying but be in better control of themselves when they are angry or violent. But controlling their emotions is all of a piece for men. It is because they are in pain and because they can cause pain that they need to control themselves. If men are emotionless and numb, it isn't because they have no emotions, it's because they have too many. Their pulse pounds in their heads. They want to strike out, to shout with rage, to overtake the object of their lust, to grieve. All these things they want to do, but they do not. If you want to be a man, you must bury your emotions and regain control. But there is no burying your bad emotions without burying them all. That is why there is no such thing as a good cry for a man.

When I was a boy, my father used to recite a nonsense riddle. Sometimes he did it to distract me when I was crying or angry.

At other times he told it to tease my brain. He always fired it off in an instant because being able to say the riddle was supposed to be more difficult than finding its answer. But I always wanted to know the answer anyway. The riddle went like this: If it takes twenty-four pancakes to shingle a doghouse, how long does it take a blindfolded mosquito with handcuffs on to knock the seeds out of a dill pickle?

One night, parked in the grass on that solitary, winding road, I concentrated on this riddle until it stumped my emotions, and then an answer came to me. I had become that ridiculous mosquito and I would never be myself again until I had knocked each and every one of the seeds out of the dill pickle. How long would it take? Only as long as it took me to realize that the white salty seeds were my teardrops and they were mine to command.

Homunculus

Where are you going, little man? Where are you going?

The ancients believed that the spermatozoon of a man held a little man who was sent into the womb of a woman, and finding it a cozy place, he ripened into a child and was brought into the world. The ancients were wrong, of course, because there are no little men inside women, only little women. There is, however, a little man stirring in the bowels of every man. Every man speaks to him when he talks to himself. Where are you going, little man? And sometimes this little man talks back. And where do you think you're going, big man?

This little man is the frightened child within, the angry child within, the child who does what other little men tell him to do even though he knows he shouldn't, because he is so small and wants to be loved. The little man pushes out a miniature scream or a muffled cry or a tiny false laugh meant to please when it's wrong to please. But this little man is also a flash of courage and bravado, an inner voice, confident and determined and prophetic. He is the little voice that responds at once and with stupefying certainty to the question, "What do you want to be when you grow up?" "A doctor." "A fireman." "An inventor." "The President of the United States." The answer to the question changes as manhood approaches, but every man knows the real answer, even if most of us are not what we want to be and never will be. The voice of a homunculus still rings in our ears. He will not go away. And we don't want him to.

Where are you going? Stay, little man. Stay. Though you may cry big blue tears, stay for a day and give me courage.

Homunculi are there to see all over the place. They are the smallness appearing in grand men who diminish themselves before our very eyes, making themselves smaller and smaller until they are mere human beings. Or they are the mere human beings inside of the men who, suddenly, by virtue of an act or a thought, acquire the heretofore unimagined bulk of a hero. The burden of public life, the habit of seeing oneself reflected in miniature in the public eye or dwarfed by the television screen, shrinks ambition in some great men, while other men, without ambition or desire, are thrust into the public eye because their smallness is too great to be contained.

Lyndon Johnson, big man, towering over so many with his tremendous nose and ears, there so small on the screen, ended it all, not because he was wrong but because he was right. I shall not run. The big man and the little man shall not run. He quit for the same reason he showed us his gallbladder scar. The little man was sewed in, right there, and with his index finger, LBJ pointed to the place where his homunculus could be found. Then he let the little man out and went to live with him and Lady Bird in Texas.

Dan Rather, little man, put on the skin of a wise man. Walter Cronkite, calm in a storm, shedding a tear only for the dead president, is the skin that Dan Rather wants to wear. It was his skin once in braver days, but he can't get it back. Everything he says is wrong; everything he says is true. He is the little man speaking in his moment of darkness and yearning and fear. It is so painful to watch him squirming on the TV screen, twisting on the hook he has set in himself, always on the verge of humiliating himself, wooden in his spontaneity. Incongruous. Courage, Dan Rather. Courage, little man.

If I were Dan Rather, I would be the same way. Before the eyes of millions, the little man must come out. It is the truth they want, after all.

It is the smallness in other men that makes them into heroes. They give up their lives because they are so small. Other lives are so big, luminescent before their eyes, souls swollen to suns, so bright and beautiful.

I am so small. I am almost nothing. I am so small. I know only one thing, one small thing, where the shutoff valve is, and I am the only one who knows where it is. It is there under ten feet of radioactive water, and the water is rising. So must have thought the Russian worker who sacrificed his life to save people farther away than his little eyes could see. The little man became a diver, tunneling downward into the waters, hand outstretched, legs twisting, back to the womb and death, into the waters of the

Chernobyl nuclear plant, as they rose up to meet the remains of the day and to cover them in poison, into the waters again to take hold of the shutoff valve, three and a half turns toward life, and the little man died so that bigger men might not.

Why did you go in there, little man? Because I am so small.

The children inside are burning alive; their lives, so huge, are blackening in the insipid heat of unworthy smoke and fire. Souls the size of the sun are burning up in a house fire. How can that be? They are all burning up, there, in those houses afire. The little men in funny red hats rush into the inferno; their lives are delicate and dry as paper, the fire is hot, and yet they rush into the inferno to take up the children, to carry them to the cool lawns. They would not do it if they were not so small, if they didn't think, "How small I am and they are so big. I will try to carry them out, though the fire is hot and they are too many for me to carry." Why do little boys want to be firemen? Because firemen, too, are little men driven by big fires.

Men for all time have envied women the power of childbirth. It is said they envy it because it is a power, and men want all the power for themselves. But what men really see in childbirth is the pouring out of the flesh and spirit within themselves, the deliverance of the little men with whom they speak and to whom they will never give birth because they could not survive the separation. Men envy women the power to deliver themselves of their inner being and to love it as another person.

After a child is born, its mother speaks to it in love and consolation; she listens to its little sounds to hear its truth and receives comfort. Every organ of sense is in communion with her child: her ears open, her eyes become powerful organs of witnessing, her mouth breathes in and tastes the bloody sweetness of new life. Then she turns to the other women in the room to speak and to receive their words, and all the words swarm to the child to swaddle it in long joyful sentences.

The father of the child doesn't say much. He looks stunned and nods his consent to the joy absentmindedly. His outward emotions and gestures replay those of the women in slow motion, as if he is trying to learn how to dance by following his partner's feet. All of his real emotions swirl within. He calls out to the little man inside to see whether he too has been delivered, and finding him in his rightful place, they whisper together in relief and wonderment, marveling about the woman there who has been untwinned and yet seems unharmed. How can she be one, they wonder, now that she is no longer two?

This is the mistake a man makes when he sees a woman give birth, why he marvels at her, why he envies her capacity and courage, because he thinks she has done something he could not want to do. Men feel kicks and turnings and voices within as surely as women do, but they don't give birth for fear of losing their insides. They fear to be emptied of cries and commands and convictions. They fear losing their guts. They are terrorized by the thought of having nothing within themselves to rely on.

Writing Life

The most profound insight of my life, the one I am most ashamed of, is that I am a better man when I am writing than when I am not. A man, for me, is someone who promises to change himself for the better, without changing himself, and who keeps his promise even if it means he will not survive it. But it is easier to imagine living well than doing it, and so my writing life brings me back again and again to an image of myself that I fail to realize in my daily life.

Writing is a bargain with yourself in which you make an appointment to meet yourself at the other side of a moment. You move into the time of writing, but you don't know whether you will keep the rendezvous with yourself in the future. Each change in the writing, each word that falls away in favor of another, each idea made true and then false by the straightness of the line is an accusation of hypocrisy against yourself. "How can you change what was true a moment ago to something else and still remain the same man? By banishing all contradiction from your writing, you may create a beautiful fable, but if it is a liar's fable, you are the liar who told it. When your true self keeps the appointment, as true selves always do, will he embrace the liar you have become? What kind of hypocrite would do that?"

Such is my inner monologue when I write—the substance of my writer's block—and it makes clear why the pact to meet yourself describes the virtues of the writing life. I think it also describes the conditions of trying to be a man. At least this is what I tell myself, since men have worried to themselves for a long time about how much they are permitted to change before they become someone else. Perhaps this explains why men have been writers in such large numbers, and why more and more women today are becoming writers as they wrestle with new identities, new obligations, and new sorrows. The promises made in writing are broken or kept, as in other walks of life, but the promiser and promised are always the same person, so that breaking a promise amounts to self-betrayal and keeping one is a matter of survival.

Bad writing tempts you to change yourself for the better and for the worse, but any change is for the worse if it betrays who you are and have been. Good writing demands only one thing: that you keep your mind on it and do it right. Every day you have to write and write until you get enough experience and enough confidence to speak the language and not chatter on in an alien syntax made up of bad lessons from school or too much self-consciousness. The point is to make the words so simple that they sing. Then the words tell you who you are, and you know the truth when you hear it. When I emerge from the time of writing with my virtue intact, I have been successful in judging my writing and myself. In my writer's vision of the good life, I meet a man on the other side of the time of writing and recognize him as the face in my mirror.

The plumber may wish to become a better plumber, the dancer a better dancer, the office worker a better office worker, the painter a better painter. When I write I want to be a better man, and I am—but only as long as I am writing. And so I design ways to write more. I awaken earlier and earlier in the morning. I stumble from bed to desk through the darkness of a house haunted by others who write only in their dreams. I drift to my chair in midafternoon, unaware until I sit down of my destination, like a man who lights a cigarette before he realizes that he needs one. I conserve in my brain a messy but metaphysical surface called my writing, where a mental pencil is always in my hand. When I drop the pencil, when I turn to meet the eyes of an inquiring child or when Jill talks to me of her daily destinations before walking out the door, when I refill my coffee cup, when the vacuum cleaner wheezes or a bird chirps—then I fall at a speed beyond knowing into duller thoughts and moods, into passions and crimes, into my imperfections, frustrations, and regrets. My anger raises its ugly head, even though I had just discovered the cure to all anger. My prejudice bristles, even though moments before I had loved all races and kinds. I am hungry or thirsty or worse. The muse departs, my eyes scale over with stupidity, and then I feel the lust to write once more and forever more.

And so I enter the time of writing: I remember a moment at dusk in the spring of 1973 when I was twenty years old. I was riding a bicycle down Orchard Street in Madison, Wisconsin, two blocks from the house where I lived with four other young men during my sophomore year of college. Perhaps my experience had something to do with the action of slowly pedaling the bicycle, which I now envision as a symbol of grace and innocence, although it was maroon and I had ridden it many times before to no grand effect. A canopy of cool green leaves folded itself over the street, and I became steadily aware of the trees, the light, and time itself. Soon, the stillness of the air, the leaves, and the moment turned to a shade of green imperceptibly different from silver. The street, my place in it, and the time of day assumed a perfect harmony, the idea of which I am unable to render except by imagining again that color, a color seen so clearly that evening but never seen before or since. I knew at that moment I would never forget the experience, although I have never understood why. Now, by describing it here, I have kept the promise of that day and its memory to myself, practicing a form of virtue that I can't manage elsewhere in my life.

I know of only one other action that matches the virtuous feelings of writing. It is when I am in the act of fixing something with a tool or making a tool. All my emotions come to a halt, except for the emotions required by the job. I enter the time of work and nothing happens in the world until I exit at the end of the job to find my work there, complete and well done. I have been virtuous, and I take pride in my work, but I am saved from the narcissism of writing because my goodness has been deposited in the work, and I can admire it there, as a painter or sculptor might, without thinking that I am admiring myself.

I suspect, though, that my feelings in work are an accident of my upbringing and not the result of a true affinity to writing, although I hope I am wrong, because I like the idea of seeing the virtue of writing as a form of repair. In repair work you must imagine the true form of things on the basis of their ruins and then find a way to restore them to working order. A writer must do the same thing if he is to find beauty in this world. It is more likely, however, that I find a state of grace in repair work because I transform myself during these brief moments on the job into the image of my father, who was more skilled at repairing things than anyone I ever saw. Of all things he knew, he knew best how to work, and he exceeded all others in the ability to sustain it. A small man, his body nevertheless took on Rodinesque proportions in work: he twisted his body as he manipulated wire, wood, or metal, fit tools to his hand, cursed the unworthy, and mixed his blood with grease and dirt without fear, tunneling deeper and deeper into the core of the job and ascending higher and higher toward the perfect vision of himself. Sometimes he appeared to work only by the solitary light of his own burning cigarette, a work light and signal lamp, tipped on his lip, articulating the defeats and triumphs of the job, drooping low almost falling, snapped to attention and accomplished, rummaging for more room in his mouth as he struggled to force a fit or to lift in a tight corner. I don't smoke. My hands know no genius. I am long, lanky, and weak. But because my father's body is the body of the consummate worker, my body and all others become his when they are successful at work. And so in his image I find, if only for an instant, a better image of myself.

I didn't become a repairman, however, and I only fool myself when I think I am good at it. I imagine my best self as a writer, and I struggle to apply to my other life the lessons of my writing life. That I can't sends me back for refuge to my writing but sours it, or at the very least, I taste some bitterness in the discrepancy between the virtues of writing and the virtues of my everyday life. I dwell most often on my vices when I am not writing, which is, I gather, a kind of writing in advance, because writing navigates between the world observed and the world of the page. Once I am writing, though, its sweetness overpowers the bitter taste of my disappointment, and I forget my vices. I forget everything.

It is, of course, a notorious fact that you can write longer than you can do anything else. Writing creates a billowing amnesia, but it is sometimes troubling: while the images of my life appear with greater color and vitality when I am writing, I lose track of my responsibility for them, because writing makes me think that

I owe my allegiance to the images of my life and not to life itself. Perhaps writing is small, and writers are only small people. We like to deal in little things: pencil stubs, scraps of paper, and punctuation marks. We fit our small intelligence into cramped places to become the proverbial big fish in the small pond. The amnesia of writing is best described as forgetting the size of the pond.

The act of writing when described by a writer always takes on heroic dimensions, no matter how humble the writer. When Augustine wrote his *Confessions,* he directed them to God, for he knew that God, whose omnipotence he had described as the ability to read better than anyone else, was bound to read his every word. When Montaigne invented the modern form of the essay, it was for the purpose of introducing himself to other people so that they might learn from his mistakes—quite a bit of hubris from the retiring and unassuming man who made bold to write "Que sais-je?" on the inner dome of his tower. He was really writing only for himself, repeating in every conceivable form the mantra of his ignorance with an accent on the "I." Jean-Jacques Rousseau gave up all pretense of writing for other people: he wrote for God and for himself, but primarily for himself, since he didn't stop writing when he came to suspect that God might be reading Voltaire. The cork-lined room of Proust is the natural habitat of writers, where nothing intrudes to contradict their image of themselves or to whisper the noise of their impotence.

The people who really influence the world never put their ideas on paper, except for an occasional memo written by another's hand. Writing is not really about influencing the world; it is about imagining the moral conditions of the heart and its ability to feel. Writers are, of course, just as happy to acquire power and fame as anyone else—perhaps more so—but when they do, they usually become worse writers because you can't peddle influence in a cork-lined room. Writers make poor politicians because they are unwilling to shake hands or kiss babies, except in their imagination, and they don't know the meaning of compromise. A compromise for a writer is only the name for a sentence awaiting further revision, not something to put into law. Nor does the art of the deal make much sense to writers, who always think too late about what the entire deck contains, so fascinated are they by the faces on the individual cards. Writers are useless in the world, unless you think that it is useful to spend vast amounts of time alone, to carry on imaginary conversations with yourself, to think of good things to say at bad moments, and of bad things at good moments, and to make all of your promises to yourself.

I have drifted from celebrating the virtues of writing to cursing its vices. But I still think I am lucky because my writing brings me face to face with the good life, which is, finally, only the chance to design your own idea of happiness and to know it when you have it. Writers are lucky to find the image of happiness in their own making, and if they are luckier still, their words make up the images by which other people try to imagine their own happiness.

We search in life for the images we need to live. We find them, if we are lucky, in our own making but always, whatever our luck, in words and dreams and memories, in books and newspapers, at the movies, on billboards, in the happy but unlikely laughter of television sitcom families, in accidental meetings—at those moments when the reality around us comes to a standstill, out of time and beyond time, to form those images that we can never truly forget but almost always fail to remember.

The last time I saw my mother was in her coffin at the funeral home. A nurse at the hospital where my mother had been on her deathbed for months had telephoned one morning to tell me that my mother's hands and feet were turning cold and she would not last the day. I set off at once on the long trip home to be at her bedside, but I arrived too late to see her alive. I had to wait two long days before she was shown, against her last wishes, in an open casket, and I could take possession of my last image of her. She looked far more beautiful in death than she had in the last months of life, but she was a different woman from the one I had known. She wore her hair in a new way, and her makeup was not to her taste. Her skin was cold, as I expected it would be, but it is hard to convey how strange it really is to have that expectation fulfilled by someone you truly love.

I had a dream last night about my mother, now many years dead. In the dream I saw her as she once had been. She was working in her garden, hunched in the beauty of her middle years and untouched by the cancer that had disfigured her in life. I came upon her as she was working over her marigolds and petunias. She was not as surprised to see me as I was to see her, unconcerned by death. I soon forgot I was speaking to a dead woman, and we talked casually in the way that people who live together talk day in and day out. I awoke from the dream not being able to remember our words, though I still long to hear them. But I do remember the image of her that day at her work, for which I am grateful—a not young but handsome woman who had the good sense and modest awareness of her own beauty to wear a veil about her face in the garden.